DATE DUE

SEP 1 3 2000			
FEB 2 9 2008			

The Courage to Care

*Seven Families
Touched by Disability and
Congregational Caring*

Judy Griffith Ransom

UPPER
ROOM BOOKS
NASHVILLE

THE COURAGE TO CARE
Seven Families Touched by Disability and Congregational Caring

Copyright © 1994 by Judy Griffith Ransom
All rights reserved.

Unless otherwise designated, scripture quotations are from the New Revised Standard Version of the Bible, copyright © 1989 by the Division of Christian Education of the National Council of Churches of Christ in the United States of America. Used by permission.

The Scripture quotation from First Corinthians on the dedicatory page comes from *The Living Bible* (Wheaton, Illinois: Tyndale House Publishers, 1971) and is used by permission.

For additional acknowledgments, see page 206.

Cover design: John Robinson
First printing: March 1994 (3)
ISBN: 0-8358-0701-0
Library of Congress Catalog Card Number: 93-60145

Printed in the United States of America

The cross on the cover is the Tau cross, the cross of healing. The Tau cross is one of the oldest crosses. It is thought that the cross Moses lifted before the Hebrews in their wilderness wanderings was a cross of this shape.

In memory of

Megan Kristine Tucky

All the special gifts and powers from God will
someday come to an end, but love goes on forever.

—1 Corinthians 13:8

Contents

Acknowledgments

I wish to thank the members of First United Methodist Church, Hendersonville, Tennessee, for the inspiration to write this book. Their gifts of love and care for hurting families create solutions where none seem to exist.

I am grateful to the individuals who have shared their stories and to their families, friends, and congregations whose love in action provides a guide.

Thank you to my agent, Charlie Flood; to my editors, Rita Collett and Dr. Lynne Deming; to school counselor, Marilyn Henderson, M.Ed., for reading the manuscript and making suggestions; to Claudia Douglass, M.S.S.W., the parent of an adult son with mental retardation, who serves on many mental retardation boards, is a lay leader in the Episcopal Diocese, and works in hospice, for adding special insights.

A sincere thank-you to
Scott, Audra, Whitney, and Tracy Ransom
and a host of family and friends
who encouraged me and believed in me.

Introduction

I BELIEVE EACH OF US IS CALLED to matter in this business of living by faithfully sharing our talents with one another. *The Courage to Care* is about searching for ways to be God's hands in action to persons with disabilities and to their families, as well as the good that comes to both giver and receiver when we are faithful to Christ's commandment to "love one another."

The birth of my great-niece Megan Tucky brought new understandings to our family about the need for a caring community. Megan, seemingly healthy at birth, began regressing at the age of one year and soon lost all of her learned skills. After nearly two years of tests by various doctors, she was diagnosed with Rett syndrome, a rare disorder that would leave her completely dependent and profoundly retarded.

At family gatherings, it was easy to see the nonstop caring that Megan's needs required: forty-five minutes to feed her a meal, constant monitoring, hours of rocking to soothe whatever made her scream. An hour or two of respite for her parents had enormous restorative powers and family members provided that easily. Too soon, Megan's parents moved halfway across the country. Now they had no family member to offer them respite. Perhaps no one in their church and neighborhood picked up on their need for a break from constant caregiving or no one knew how to offer help.

I began to think about others in similar circumstances who were far from traditional support networks. I reflected on the impact that a few caring persons could have on their quality of life. I chose to write *The Courage to Care* in response to Megan. I hope it will serve as a guide for congregations, neighbors, friends, and even strangers who want to help in time of crisis but aren't quite sure where or how they could fit in.

More than forty million persons in the United States have a disability. The gift of care can create margins that allow time for self-care and refreshment for caregivers, that decrease isolation, and that increase a feeling of connectedness and community. The gift of care comes in many small packages: an hour of reading to someone living in isolation, books transcribed in pencil for someone allergic to printer's ink, an hour of stimulation exercise for a child with Down's syndrome, a look through old photo albums with a man with Alzheimer's disease, an hour of rocking for a distressed youngster, forty-five minutes to feed and coax eye contact from a child with autism, thirty minutes of strengthening exercises with a young man with a head injury, a Saturday to build a wheelchair ramp or widen a doorway.

This book records the stories of seven ordinary families, each with a member with a disability, whose lives were changed dramatically by ordinary congregations, friends, and neighbors who had the courage to care. Perhaps the responses of the people in this book are similar to responses you could make. Perhaps you will see a way to reach out a hand of care to change someone's world. ❖

Jason

OH, WONDERFUL! RUTH SAID TO HERSELF as the senior minister introduced Stan Carder, the new youth pastor, to the congregation her first Sunday back at church. He seemed articulate and committed, and those qualities shone even stronger as Stan spoke to the young adult Sunday school class. After class, Ruth welcomed Stan to her home church. "We're so glad you're here," Ruth said. A twenty-seven-year-old elementary school teacher, Ruth had rented an apartment and moved back to Billings, Montana, that very week. She was single, happy, and content. She had no plans to marry.

"I'm glad I'm here too," Stan replied. Stan's easygoing personality suited his work as a youth pastor. He was a quiet listener in times of crisis, unafraid of being present to people who were suffering. At the same time he had an energy and a love of fun and life that made him an exciting companion.

Stan and Ruth soon discovered they shared a love of the outdoors and began to take long drives to a favorite restaurant, then up to Ruth's family's cattle ranch. Ruth was an excellent equestrian and taught Stan to ride on the spacious ranch, sharing childhood memories of her life in Montana. They dated eighteen months and became engaged on Ruth's birthday.

Stan and Ruth made a striking bride and groom. Both were tall and slender with dark brown hair. They were so comfortable with themselves that it was easy to laugh and smile, which they did often—and dream. Their relationship was a sharing one. Ruth could easily share her feelings with Stan, and he felt the same way. They held nothing back. Ruth's family, which included Ruth's mom and dad, brother Dwight and his wife Sue, sister Elaine and her husband Ted, had warmly welcomed Stan. All of her family members lived on a Livingston, Montana, cattle ranch.

STAN DROVE HIS CAR INTO THE DUSTY KOA CAMPGROUND, watching for Steve Koontz with whom he would interview as a candidate for the senior pastor position at the Paradise Valley Church. All around him church members were pulling picnic baskets out of cars. Steve's approach on a borrowed motorcycle was impossible to miss with a trail of dust kicked up behind him. Somehow the motorcycle got away from him, and Steve was thrown. He injured his head and banged up the rest of himself too. Stan jumped right into the pastoral role, going to the hospital to sit with Steve.

"Thanks for coming," Steve said as the orderlies wheeled him to a room. He was staying overnight for observation.

Stan smiled. "I'm more than happy to be here," he said honestly. Someone had once asked him, "Where's your parish?" Stan had replied, "Anybody and everybody; my ministry is people."

Stan did become the church's new pastor. He set to work developing a program of Bible verse memorization called AWANA, which stood for Approved Work[ers] Are Not Ashamed. The program helped individuals have scripture available to them as a life reference because they committed verses to memory. The church honored participants each year for their efforts.

"What's troubling you?" Ruth asked after church one day.

"I've been thinking about Jerry. He participates in the Special Olympics each year, and I think it would be good for him and for the church to honor his efforts, just like we do for the kids in AWANA. He needs recognition too."

A few Sundays later, Jerry walked proudly to the front of the church where Stan stood holding three shiny medals. Stan explained that Jerry, then in his thirties, had been born with Down's syndrome and participated each year in the Special Olympics, an athletic competition for persons with disabilities held around the country. "We are here to honor Jerry for his fine efforts," Stan said. He announced the name of each event in which Jerry had participated and hung the medals, one by one, around Jerry's neck. The church members burst into applause. Jerry threw his shoulders back, waved at the crowd, and threw kisses.

STAN'S SCHEDULE WAS FULL BOTH AS A PASTOR AND A FATHER. He and Ruth were the parents of three-year-old Kim and seven-year-old Jeremy when they learned Ruth was pregnant with their third child.

Their time of waiting flew by. June 29, 1981 started out as a normal day. It was almost the Fourth of July, and firecrackers were popping in anticipation of the holiday already. Ruth picked up the phone and called her sister, who lived about sixty miles away. "Elaine, we're going to the hospital."

"I'll meet you there," Elaine promised.

Stan and Ruth drove the sixty miles to Bozeman in an hour, happily anticipating the birth of their child. Their baby was born at 10:30 A.M., an hour after their arrival at the hospital.

"You've got a beautiful son," the doctor announced to Stan and Ruth, holding him up for them to see.

At that moment, life was full of promise for this baby. A few minutes later, Stan stepped into the hallway to give Elaine the happy news.

"It's a boy. He's just beautiful," Stan announced happily.

"See, the Lord loves you—he's perfect," Elaine said.

"Mr. Carder." Stan turned around, alarmed at something in the doctor's tone of voice.

The warm sense of joy that filled the delivery room was shattered in the next moment. The nurse discovered that Jason had no rectal opening when she tried to check his temperature, and suddenly the baby that had a lifetime of promise ahead of him was dying. After wrapping the baby in warm blankets, the nurse handed him to Ruth. At first glance the baby they'd named Jason had none of the Down's syndrome features, but now discussion arose as to whether Jason did indeed have Down's. While one doctor and nurse were supportive, a second nurse was blunt.

"He's so cute. I didn't think he had all of these problems. Don't worry, you can have another baby."

"A life flight airplane from Salt Lake City, Utah, is flying in to take Jason to a hospital with specialists who will build his intestinal structure surgically," the doctor told them.

"I'm going," Ruth announced from the delivery room table.

"There won't be room on the plane," she was told.

Stan's and Ruth's eyes met. They were determined to go. Together the couple dedicated Jason in prayer to the Lord. Then Stan rushed out of the delivery room toward the pay phone in the waiting room. The doctor had warned them that Jason probably wouldn't survive the flight. Stan's hands shook as he inserted a quarter and dialed Tom Peterson, a pilot friend.

"I need you to fly us somewhere," Stan said, explaining the situation.

"I'll be right there," Tom agreed.

"Give us a couple of hours; a plane is flying in for Jason."

Then Stan called home to explain what was happening and suggested that Ruth's mom and dad bring Kim and Jeremy to the airport. Within hours of the birth, the three siblings met for a few brief moments, then Jason was whisked away. The family passed along information to people in the church, and several had called to let Stan and Ruth know that their prayers were with them.

As a medical team loaded Jason into the plane in Bozeman, a nurse explained the admittance paperwork she held out to Stan for his signature. A sense of unreality surrounded Stan and Ruth as Tom's Cessna 185 roared down the runway and then lifted off into the blue sky, heading southwest toward Salt Lake City. Jason had been born at 10:30 A.M. Now, three hours later, Ruth was back in her maternity slacks and blouse, huddled in the backseat as the plane rattled and shuddered.

"ARE YOU STAN CARDER?" A MAN ASKED AS STAN AND RUTH sat alone in the hospital admissions waiting room.

"Yes."

"Sign this please," he said, holding out a piece of paper.

"I really don't sign things without reading them," Stan said.

"Sign this please," the man repeated.

Stan signed it and received an air ambulance bill for $4,000. The bill was stamped "paid in full." Stan later found out that twelve anonymous businessmen put money into an account for use when high-risk babies were dying.

Stan had called to ask, "Who do we thank?" and was told, "You don't thank anybody." Stan was dumbfounded. It was a lesson in cherishing. The businessmen valued Jason's life just because he was a human baby. Period.

Reactions to Jason varied, creating a rise and fall within Stan's and Ruth's emotions. Persons' compassion generated thankfulness and hope; persons' harsh, insensitive remarks created anger.

"Well, are your other kids normal?" an intern asked as they stared helplessly at their tiny, bald baby who was crying in obvious distress.

"Would you like to hold your baby?" a kindly nurse asked, and Ruth burst into tears.

"No," said Ruth, afraid to hold Jason. He was so fragile looking, and she wasn't sure she could hold him without damaging or rearranging tubes or hurting him physically. The environment of sterile surroundings—needles, wires, beeps from monitoring machines—and the eerie feeling of illness, disability, and death shrouded her perception that a real baby was lying there in need.

Ruth wanted to pull away and leave him lying there so as not to bother him or to acknowledge that it was her baby who was having troubles in his early, brief life. Ruth and Stan had scrubbed up and put on green sterile gowns, but it was hard to want to touch a baby that looked so foreign.

The nurse gently lifted Jason out of the isolette. "You will hold your baby," she said firmly. She took the necessary step to relieve their fear and apprehension. Ruth sat down in the rocking chair beside Jason's isolette and held out her arms. She looked into Jason's face; and instead of seeing the wires and the monitors, she saw a smooth, pink baby with just the beginnings of soft blond eyebrows beneath the barest wisp of blond hair. His tiny eyes were tightly shut, but she could see that he had eyelashes. His lungs were well formed; he was howling. Automatically she held him close and felt his tiny fingers move in hers while his infinitesimally small feet gave a surprisingly strong kick. She traced the curve of his ear with her finger, kissed him lightly on the cheek and placed him in Stan's waiting arms. Jason was only a person with problems. He was alive, warm, breathing, and very dependent. Holding him helped her get over her initial fear, although she remained very uncertain.

As they held Jason, a surgeon entered the room. "I am Dr. Michael Matlack. I understand you are a pastor. I am a Christian too. I'm a surgeon here, and I attend the First Evangelical Free Church. I'm going to save your son's life. Could you please come with me for a few minutes? I am going to tell you exactly what I am going to do."

He began to diagram the surgical procedure he would use to build Jason's rectal structure. Suddenly he stopped and looked at Ruth. "And who are you?" he asked.

"I'm Mrs. Carder."

"And what are you doing here? You just gave birth to a baby." Concerned about her physical condition, the doctor suggested that Ruth go home and not come back.

"I'm staying with my baby," she said resolutely. "I'm sorry to have to ask you this question, but I have to know. Is Jason's life valuable to you? Are you going to do as much for him in surgery as you would for a normal child, or is this just an experiment that you would conduct on a child?"

In the last few hours, Ruth and Stan had heard the word *handicap* many times. It sounded as if a baby with a handicap was not a real person. The physician's attitude concerned them. The doctor's assurance brought a measure of comfort.

Jason's surgery was successful, and he joined four other high-risk infants in a room. Because the hospital was a children's hospital, thirty other high-risk infants, and children who had been in accidents, filled the unit. The Carders' own upset was compounded by the grief and the upset of other distraught parents. Ruth felt guilty because Jason looked so good. Other parents' children were having brain surgery or heart surgery; Jason might only have Down's syndrome.

Without their own support network, Stan's and Ruth's spirits sank lower and lower. The only constant in their crisis was God. The couple found that God's presence was with them in Salt Lake City, Utah, just as God had been with them in Montana. Their understanding of that presence and the warmth of friends supported and sustained them.

Stan called Al, his former college roommate, the only person he knew in Salt Lake. Al was out of town with his family, but a girl who was house-sitting offered to relay Stan's request. Al's response was, "*The* Stan Carder? Yeah, tell him to use the house as long as he likes."

THE DRIVE ACROSS MONTANA, DOWN THROUGH THE CORNER of Wyoming and into Utah, flew by for Elaine and Ted, Ruth's sister and brother-in-law. "I'm glad you're an expoliceman," Elaine said, as Ted sipped coffee and kept his eyes on the black strip of highway that lay ahead.

"Just a few more hours, honey, and we'll be there," Ted replied.

When Elaine and Ted stepped off the elevator into the antiseptic smell of the neonatal unit, they had no way of knowing what they would find. *Had Jason survived the flight? What state of mind would Ruth and Stan be in? What could they possibly say to a couple that had just had their hopes and dreams dashed?*

Ted and Elaine didn't know the answer to any of those questions. They only knew that Stan and Ruth needed their support, rather than having to face some of the worst moments of their life alone. If family ever needed to be present, it was now.

"I can't believe you're here," Ruth gasped, jumping up from her chair in Jason's room with a start.

Elaine and Ted looked at each other and grinned. It was a thrill for them to see the reaction of joy and relief their arrival brought to Stan and Ruth.

"Jason?" Elaine asked her sister quietly.

"He's okay. He's going to be okay," Ruth answered. "But we still don't know if he has Down's syndrome."

All of Elaine and Ted's wondering about what they would say disappeared.

"What about the ranch?" Stan asked Ted.

"No problem. Dwight agreed that we needed to get down here. He said he'd manage without me," Ted answered.

While still at the hospital, tests revealed that Jason did have an extra chromosome. The hospital geneticist broke the news to Stan and Ruth that Jason had Down's syndrome and that he would have mental retardation. Ruth thought Jason was a child with no future—a blob of flesh that would have no personality and no abilities.

Some hospitals or The ARC (formerly known as the Association of Retarded Citizens), a national organization on mental retardation, offer to pair up new parents with a "support parent," a parent whose child has had similar problems. The support parent can provide information and reassurance and be a sounding board as well as a coping model. This type of help could have relieved many of Stan's and Ruth's anxieties about Jason's possibilities for a happy life.

It was hard to look at Jason as a child after hearing *genetic accident* so many times. The words put a barrier between parent and child and created a negative feeling. *Who wants to take home an accident? What good can come out of an accident?* Ruth purposely put those thoughts out of her mind. Although she believed Jason did not have much of a future, she did believe that Jason was a child formed by God and that God had given him to them.

Having persons to laugh and cry with, persons to share with and be honest with, was important to Stan and Ruth. Elaine and Ted's presence gave them an opportunity to share their feelings without covering up anything. They were excellent listeners, allowing Stan and Ruth to say whatever they wanted. Because of their close relationship, Ted and Elaine held Ruth and Stan accountable for faulty thoughts and ideas, helping them sort through what was false and true. With them, it was okay to grieve their great expectations of future goals and desires for their son.

Ruth was breast-feeding Jason, but the combination of anesthesia and a poor sucking reflex made Jason want to fall asleep instead. "Let me help," Elaine offered, grabbing Jason's foot and slapping it gently, working to keep him awake. A poor sucking reflex often indicates developmental delay for high-risk babies, and they often nurse very slowly. Slapping Jason's feet helped him to stay awake and be successful.

"Hey Dumbo, stay awake," Elaine said, then stopped.

Ruth looked at her sister and when their eyes met, they both burst out laughing.

"Dumbo might not be the right nickname for a Down's baby, but we can't live our lives being soooo careful," Ruth said reassuringly.

Stan and Ruth realized that they would have to help Jason fit into their family instead of changing their lifestyle to accommodate him, becoming fanatical about language or words with double meanings.

After nursing, Jason slept soundly in his isolette. Elaine turned to Ruth and said, "You know, you really do need to get away from here for a little while. Stan, she needs to get out. Life will go on." Elaine, who felt Ruth was so giving, now seized the opportunity to do something special for Ruth. For three days Ruth had worn the same billowing maternity slacks and top.

"I'm taking you shopping for a new outfit," Elaine insisted as Ruth started to protest. Now that they knew Jason would recover, it would help Ruth's outlook to leave the hospital for a few hours. Elaine was delighted to be able to do something to lift Ruth's spirits.

"It's a relief to change clothes and look sharp again and to eat something other than hospital food," Ruth said as she and Elaine finished lunch that afternoon. It was refreshing to eat in an attractive restaurant instead of a drab cubicle, to view something other than sickness, to hear laughter instead of groans and crying, to see blue sky and green grass. As the sisters walked arm in arm back to the car, Ruth lifted her head and took a deep breath.

"What are you doing?" Elaine asked.

Ruth smiled. "Feeling the breeze on my face instead of air conditioning." Just getting out of the hospital for a few hours gave Ruth a more positive attitude. When they returned to the hospital, Ruth felt energized.

"Nice suit," Stan said with a grin, pleased to see Ruth return his smile. He had to admit that the deep blue, crisp outfit looked a lot better than Ruth's crumpled maternity slacks and shirt.

"I see they've put you fellas to work," returned Elaine. The two men were sitting on chairs, cutting out donut-shaped colostomy patches. A nurse had showed them how; and as Stan showed Ruth, they began the first steps of assuming responsibility for the care of their child. A special nurse arrived to teach the couple exactly how to care for Jason's colostomy. It wasn't simple, but they were building a new set of skills and their anxiety about handling this fragile baby decreased a little.

That night Ted and Elaine watched Jason sleeping while Stan and Ruth stretched their legs in the hallway. "The greatest gift to a mother is to love her child," Elaine said.

WITH THE BIRTH OF THEIR BABY, RUTH AND STAN WONDERED how to explain Jason's physical condition to their son, Jeremy. Kim, their daughter, was too young to fully understand what mental retardation might mean to Jason, but Jeremy could. "What will Jeremy think of God?" Stan worried, remembering their fervent prayers for a "normal" baby. Ruth and Stan agreed to wait awhile to share the news with the children, while they concentrated on caring for Jason's physical needs.

Most children who are seven or eight still think pretty concretely. For most, these kinds of theological questions won't trouble them. But Jeremy and Kim felt bad that Jason was frail and tiny and had already had to go through so much surgery in his short life.

"He's so cute," Kim told her mother one day. "His fingers are so small and yellow. They look just like french fries."

The children loved to stand over Jason's bassinet and shake a rattle for him or just slip their larger fingers into his hand and wait for him to curl his fingers around theirs. And they did their best to be quiet so that both their mom and their baby brother could rest.

After a month, Stan and Ruth told the children that Jason had Down's syndrome. "What's that?" Jeremy asked.

"He's going to be like Jerry at our church," Stan explained.

"That's okay, I'll love him anyhow," Jeremy replied with seven-year-old candor. In fact, children usually have a much easier time accepting a disabled sibling than their parents do because they do not have to grieve the loss of all the hopes and expectations they had for the baby. With honest communication and adequate interpretation of circumstances, siblings usually adjust well.

As the weeks went by, Ruth and Stan noticed the difference between the celebration of the births of Jeremy and Kim and that of Jason. No bevy of well-wishers welcomed Jason home; no flowers, booties, gowns, and soft blankets conveyed the message, "Welcome, we're glad you are here."

Ruth's heart ached for somebody to say, "Ohhhh, let me hold him," but they didn't. No one outside her family talked to Jason like they did her other babies, and it hurt. Everyone seemed to view Jason as a problem, invalidating him as a person of importance. Ruth felt isolated by the special needs of her child, and she sometimes wondered if anyone could understand what she was going through.

At night, Jason did not sleep well. Ruth began to feel the pull of responsibilities to family, church, and home stretching her reserves. While friends did not know exactly what they were going through, people did begin to step in to make certain that she and Stan had some time to get to know each other again. It was fun just to go out and eat a good meal that Ruth did not have to prepare, to share a quiet evening together.

A young nurse, hearing that Jason had a colostomy, offered, "Let me come and take care of him while you get out. I know how to take care of a colostomy." Ruth had been reluctant to let others care for him because of the colostomy and the standoffishness of those who didn't want to hold him for that reason. She felt comfortable accepting this offer and planned a dinner out with Stan. She needed the break, and the nurse seemed to enjoy visiting with the older children as well.

"I'd love to come and stay again," the nurse told them. Stan and Ruth agreed that would be helpful and took her up on her offer.

Kim and Jeremy needed Ruth's attention too. They wanted to work on crafts, to color, and to read with her. It took time to push Kim on the swing, give her baths, and drive Jeremy to friends' houses to play. Jeremy had lashed out angrily a few times when he felt Jason was getting more attention that he deserved, and Ruth worked to maintain a balance for all of the children.

THE CARDERS WERE REALIZING THAT A DISABILITY AFFECTS EVERYONE in a family. Jeremy and Kim, while they did not grieve Jason's future, had to adjust to the extra time and attention that Jason required.

An organized, outgoing individual who was used to being the "doer," Ruth was so private about her own needs that no one realized how tired she was getting. As the pastor's wife, she had jumped back into her duties of running the women's ministries. Now, beyond taking care of her two other children so they wouldn't become jealous or feel left out, she had to put in the suggested number of hours for Jason's stimulation exercises. The exercises helped him increase muscle tone and explore his environment.

At prayer circle one afternoon, someone asked Ruth, "What would you like us to pray for?"

Her emotional reserves gone, Ruth was able to be honest. "Please pray for me, for an improvement in my morale. I just can't do everything." Then the words came pouring out, "I will have to come clean. I just can't do it anymore."

The group members were heartbroken that they hadn't picked up on Ruth's struggles. Ruth's openness and vulnerability gave them an opportunity to build a new relationship with her and Jason, and they assertively offered their help.

When Ruth began to protest, someone reassured her. "I know you are tired, and the house needs cleaning. My house needs it too. What day shall I come?" The way they took over clearly conveyed their desire to help.

BECKY BANSTRA, Ruth's friend, came to Ruth and said, "I would love to come one day a week and do the infant stimulation program with Jason. I'm not afraid of a child with a disability."

Becky went along with what Ruth was doing with Jason. The instructor from the county program came and spent an hour showing Becky the movements Jason needed to be put through. It wasn't difficult, just time consuming. While Becky helped Jason with rolling over or balancing or sitting-up activities, Ruth was able to do an activity that was important to her. While Becky rolled Jason down a bolster, Ruth could do a chore without interruption. Becky could help Jason experience his environment by bouncing him on her knee, tickling him to help him tighten his stomach muscles, rolling him from side to side, helping him reach for an object and manipulate it.

Because significantly delayed children do not interact spontaneously with their environment, parents need to be their primary teacher and initiate interaction. Half of mental development occurs by the age of six, so Jason's early years were critically important. Not only did Becky help Jason get a solid start, she came to realize just how much help he needed to interact with his world.

Becky now understood why Ruth struggled to get her housework done, direct the church choir, take care of her children, and relate to her husband. As her understanding of life with Jason increased, Becky's expectations of Ruth became realistic. When Becky gave Ruth the gift of time for self-care by caring for Jason, she also gave the family the gift of a refreshed mother and wife who was warm and relaxed instead of tense and hurried.

Becky's visits also provided her daughter, AMY, an opportunity to see how to treat a child with a disability. The Carder family treated Jason as valuable and loved. At the age of eleven, Amy enjoyed spending time with Jason and even came to the Carders by herself to visit and play with him. When she entered high school, Amy gave a speech on Down's syndrome, supplying her classmates with new insights into the great capacity that individuals with Down's syndrome have to love without being judgmental.

Amy minored in special education at college and found employment at a school for disabled children. She now works with 150 children, most with Down's syndrome, in a swimming program. Through Jason, Amy was drawn to children with Down's, children she finds lovable and fun to be around.

Amy, like all people, received both negative and positive messages as she grew up. Through her relationship with Jason, Amy experienced acceptance for who she was, which led to her discovery of a career that would give her enjoyment and fulfillment for years to come.

THE FIRST YEAR AND A HALF OF JASON'S LIFE had been filled with adjustments and balancing. Jason had undergone a third surgery to repair his rectal structure in Salt Lake City over the Thanksgiving holidays. RICK and SHEILA, a couple they had met at the hospital during Jason's first operation, had brought their small trailer to the hospital for Stan and Ruth to use as a retreat. Their baby had been born with spina bifida, and they understood the need for a place to get away from the hospital during long confinements. A knock on Jason's door interrupted Stan and Ruth's debate about a pressed turkey dinner in the hospital cafeteria.

"Come in," Stan called, wondering who would be visiting on this family holiday.

"Happy Thanksgiving," Rick greeted them. He then suggested, "Let's walk out to the trailer."

"I was just about to take Ruth to the cafeteria," Stan said.

"Let's go out to the trailer first," Rick said. "Grab a coat; it's freezing out."

The threesome slogged through the wet, cold parking lot toward Rick's small trailer, which was lit by a single light bulb. "Go on in," Rick directed. Stan and Ruth opened the door. Before them sat a turkey roasted to perfection, with stuffing and all the trimmings and a table set for two—a reminder that someone cared.

THROUGHOUT JASON'S RECOVERY from his November 1982 surgery, Stan grieved both Jason's pain and his own. He felt bad for Jason who'd had three surgeries and was still a toddler. And he was overcome with his own disillusionment and bitterness over a future that was lost to his son. One night after church, Ruth confronted her husband. "Honey, do you love Jason? Because until you can honestly thank God for him, you will never be free of the pain."

At home Stan prayed, "Lord, make me willing to thank you for Jason." That night Stan finally felt free of the grief that had plagued him.

Ruth had decided she could take one of two roads with Jason. She could choose the road of bitterness and anger, which destroys; or she could choose the road of happiness and peace, which causes joy.

She believed in 1 Thessalonians 5:18: "Give thanks in all circumstances; for this is the will of God in Christ Jesus for you."

After working out his gratitude and thankfulness, Stan was looking forward to a summer vacation with the family. School was ending and Steve Koontz, Stan's motorcycle friend from the church, invited Stan to ride along with him to pick up some construction materials.

"I've bought some concrete forms in Kansas City. Would you like to go and share some of the driving?" Steve asked.

Stan worked for Steve whenever Steve needed help. Stan had been instrumental in the growth of Steve's Christian life through his message from the pulpit. But Steve felt Stan's influence even more through Stan's ministry as an ambulance chaser. When tragedy hit their valley—and it had, with sixteen members of the valley buried in the past eighteen months and only one from a natural death—it was important to have someone like Stan around who could be with someone who was hurting.

When they'd talked about it, Stan had explained, "When people are in an intensive care situation you earn the right to speak. You earn the right because you build a friendship, a relationship with them. The main thing is to listen, listen, listen. I am coming to understand the call to weep with those who weep and to rejoice with those who rejoice."

Stan knew that he did not have to "fix" anything for those he came to comfort; and in fact, they did not want him to. He knew that it was okay for people to struggle. "I've learned to take all the time in the world to be tender with an individual who is hurting," Stan said, and Steve remembered the day that Stan sat quietly with him at the hospital after his motorcycle wreck.

"People whose loved one is dying have a whole life passing before them—all of their memories. You need a holy sensitivity, a willingness to impart the gospel of God."

The morning for Stan to accompany Steve arrived. "Say hello to your folks for me," Ruth said, as Stan climbed into Steve's big rig. Part of the reason Stan wanted to go to Kansas City was to visit his parents. But Stan also welcomed the chance to drive Steve's big truck and visit with his friend.

When Stan and Steve had disappeared from sight, Ruth called to Jeremy and Kim, "Let's forget the last day of school. Would you like to go up to the ranch instead?"

Their shouts of enthusiasm were all the answer she needed.

AFTER A GREAT OVERNIGHT VISIT WITH STAN'S FOLKS, the two men headed home with their load of forms. They planned to drive straight through without stopping, and Stan climbed into the sleeper compartment of the truck as Steve swung onto the Topeka exit. Just as Stan closed his eyes, he felt the truck sliding out of control on the slippery ramp. With a loud crash, the truck flipped over, landing on its top. Uninjured, Steve climbed out and shouted for Stan.

"I'm wedged in between the air conditioner," Stan called.

"Don't worry, buddy. The fire trucks are on their way," Steve said, staying close by.

While Stan hung upside down, a gray-haired man in his late fifties poked his head in to the sleeper compartment and commanded Stan, "Son, don't you move a muscle. And I mean, don't move!"

Within twenty minutes of the crash, Stan was cut loose, placed on a gurney board, and taken to an area hospital by ambulance.

"You were lucky," the doctor told him frankly. "Your neck is broken at the base of your brain. Two more millimeters, and you would have died." Stan's mind flashed back to the gray-haired stranger whom he had not seen since the time of the accident.

When Steve learned the extent of Stan's injuries, he found a telephone and dialed Ruth.

"Ruthie, there's been an accident," he told her.

"Should I come?" Ruth asked, immediately realizing the blessing God had bestowed by having her in the right place—with her mother, sister, and brother.

"It's probably a good idea if you get down here," Steve said.

Ruth arranged a flight to Topeka where Stan's parents met her. Stan was in his room when she arrived at the hospital. He had six broken ribs and a damaged lung, but it was his broken neck that devastated Ruth. One month earlier her sister-in-law's brother had died of a broken neck, and Stan had officiated at his funeral. She spent the night in prayer, "You took us through Jason and gave us peace and joy with him. You've promised peace and joy sufficient. You must take care of Stan, Lord, because I can't do it."

Four days after the accident, Stan had surgery to bolt a steel "halo" into his skull to stabilize his spine. The four bolts connected to a steel ring that encircled his head. The steel ring was attached to shoulder turnbuckles on a form-fitted plastic and wool vest.

At the hospital, Stan was in excruciating pain. Some nights he stayed up all night. By the time Stan returned home, the pain was manageable, but he couldn't tolerate any noise or activity around him. The children spent the first month on the ranch with their aunts and uncles and grandmother while Stan recuperated at home. The church reached out with a prayer chain, and cards poured in. Stan kept the cards as a reminder of their care.

FIVE WEEKS AFTER THE ACCIDENT, STAN FELT READY to preach. "As you can see, I'm wearing a halo. Unfortunately my doctors won't let me drive for a while," he told the congregation his first Sunday back at church. "I'm sorry I won't be able to get around to visit."

DIANA CHASE, an older woman sitting in the congregation that morning, was struck by the regret in Stan's voice about his inability to visit his flock. Diana had begun attending the church recently; and although she was not a person who volunteered a lot, she felt the time was right for her to reach out.

Diana's son had died earlier that year. As her pastor, Stan had helped her make sense of her suffering. Stan had given her the name of a woman who lived nearby who also had lost a son. "You have a lot in common," Stan had told her. "I believe you would bring comfort to each other." Diana had taken Stan's suggestion and in time had become close friends with the woman.

"Stan, I'd be glad to drive you around the valley so you can visit," Diana offered after church.

"That would be helpful," Stan agreed. "I'll let you know." Visiting in the valley required driving forty-five miles a day just to get around to a few houses. That afternoon Ruth and Stan talked it over and agreed that was Diana's ministry.

A few days later, Diana Chase stopped by Stan's home to pick him up. She was an outsider in a church with many longtime members. Driving Stan gave her a stronger sense of belonging. Stan and Ruth had supported her during her bereavement, and now she was grateful to be a part of the ministry of Paradise Valley Church.

After several visits, Stan suggested they stop in Bozeman at a truck stop that served delicious soups, followed by a trip to the local Christian bookstore where he was able to suggest a version of the New Testament to Diana. She could only imagine the stress that wearing a steel "halo" bolted into your skull must create. Stan too was aware of the stares and whispers the contraption generated. He was beginning to know what it felt like to be physically "different."

Others in the community also reached out to Stan in his pain. MIKE ART at the Chico Hot Springs Resort invited Stan to come soak in the hot springs pool. The constant ninety-degree temperature offered relief from the painful muscle spasms he suffered. Another friend called to say he had a Jacuzzi that Stan was welcome to use anytime to ease the pain from his six broken ribs.

Each person who reached out to Stan in his pain also lifted his morale, but Stan's son Jeremy put it all into perspective. At home one night, Stan had finished soaking in a hot tub of water but could not get any relief. He was miserable and his son sensed it.

"Daddy, do you want me to rub your neck?"

"That's okay, son—go ahead and play."

"Daddy . . . all I have is time," Jeremy said, refusing to budge.

STAN LEANED BACK IN HIS OFFICE CHAIR, LISTENING CAREFULLY to an old friend. "How would you like to come to California and head up our special ministries program at Grace Church?" he asked. He went on to explain that the church provided services for 200 individuals with physical and/or mental disabilities.

"I don't have the education," Stan said honestly.

"We'll supply the education; you have the experience."

Ruth and Stan prayed about their decision. They felt that the Lord had led them through a time of special preparation for this new opportunity in their lives. So they said yes.

Stan would never completely recover from his broken neck. The doctor had warned him that he could no longer carry his heavy backpack on long hiking trips, take part in aggressive sports or tumbling, and he must stay out of confining places—like working beneath a car.

Stan was able to get on with his life without bitterness. "I learned to accept my broken neck, because I accepted my son," Stan said. "The good that happened in the first two years of Jason's life led to my call to Grace Church. Through our experiences with Jason, we have learned what it is to love unconditionally. As our needs have been met by others, we accept the blessing of other people's care. Through the body of Christ, we use the gifts God gives. We've learned God is sovereign and in control; that is a wonderful source of encouragement. Nothing happens that has not been filtered through the hands of God."

STAN'S NEW CHURCH, GRACE COMMUNITY CHURCH, in Sun Valley, California, was only twenty minutes from their home in the scenic San Fernando Valley near Los Angeles. Thirty or more parking spots marked *handicapped* encircled the church. Gradually sloping ramps into the building attested to the church's commitment to accessibility.

The move brought family adjustments. Instead of wide open spaces, their new home was wedged in between two others with just a few feet on either side. Expensive housing only allowed for a three-bedroom home, which meant that Jeremy and Jason had to share a bedroom.

Stan and Ruth had committed themselves to helping Jason become as fully functioning as he could be. They treated him like they treated their other children and developed normal home relationships. For Jason, the most important feeling was that of being accepted, loved, and needed in their home. When the family went out, Jason went along.

At their new church, a woman who learned that Jason had Down's suggested a horseback riding program for kids with disabilities. "The horse is four paced instead of two paced, and that helps stimulate the brain and physical coordination," she explained. "When you develop the major motor skills, the other things will come along."

By that time, doctors had diagnosed Jason as having mild mental retardation. The idea that Jason would be a blob was only a dark memory, replaced with a more realistic outlook. At age four, Jason did not speak plainly and had some hearing impairment, but he had good coordination. He delighted in the equestrian therapy, as did his whole family. Jason had a flair for performing and was invited to appear in a few horse shows that demonstrated the success of equestrian therapy. He was always the hit of the show in his white starched shirt and chocolate brown pants.

In the audience, Jeremy and Kim talked aloud about their brother who was out in the ring. Jason first rode with no hands. He then rode lying down, standing up, and finished by doing a somersault on the back of the huge horse.

"Is that your brother?" nearby watchers asked.

The children grinned and nodded as Jason slid off the back of the horse. Everyone was proud. The horseback riding not only improved Jason's coordination but also his speech.

At home one night, Stan and Ruth felt their concern at having the boys room together with seven years difference in their ages turn to pride as they listened at their door.

"Who is this?" Jeremy asked.

Peeking inside they saw Jeremy and Jason lying across the bed, looking through a family album.

"Ewayne."

"Where is this?"

"Ranch."

"Who is this?"

"Jesus."

"CAN YOU DO THIS?" demands a blonde-haired, blue-eyed Jason as the bell for recess rings in his sixth grade special education classroom. Climbing on the jungle gym outside, he swings from one end to the other, flips upside down, and hangs his feet through the bars. Quickly a group of sixth-grade boys haul themselves up on the bars, and soon all are hanging upside down.

Jason is mainstreamed into a school with both special education and regular classrooms. Where appropriate, Jason and other special education students attend classes in regular classrooms. When recess ends, Jason shouts a good-bye to his friends as they head back to class. With his shoulders back and head up, he swaggers to the school office to run the copy machine for the rest of the afternoon.

"Hello Jason, I've got some envelopes for you to stuff," one of the school teachers says, setting a box of envelopes and letters down beside him. Jason gets to work. Later he'll make copies for other teachers. Several times a week he will work in the school cafeteria, water plants, and lead the salute to the flag. All of these activities teach him job responsibility and give him pride in accomplishing work. The goal for Jason is to find employment when he finishes school.

"Great job, Jason," his teacher, Ms. Owens, says as he shows her his completed tasks.

"Thank you," Jason replies. His chest swells just a bit with pride. Other students moving in and out of the office are no longer surprised at Jason's abilities. He has showed them that he is up to the task of getting his work done.

The goal for any child, disabled or not, is to achieve his or her fullest potential. Jason has academic ability. He can print all of the alphabet and can copy words and sentences. In math Jason uses a calculator to solve one-digit subtraction and addition problems.

The school system uses a community-based curriculum to teach recreation leisure skills to students with disabilities. Jason can use a Walkman tape recorder and is developing the ability to entertain himself.

One afternoon when Ruth came early to pick Jason up, his teacher told her, "Mrs. Carder, you know Jason is so different—he is so happy. It is clear that your family loves him and accepts him."

Ruth smiled at Jason's teacher. "We believe Jason is a gift from God, not a genetic accident. He has augmented our family, not subtracted from it."

JEREMY SLIPPED QUIETLY INTO THE HOUSE and flopped on his bed. Jason, having done his evening chore of setting the table and finishing his school work, was now playing Nintendo in the corner of their shared bedroom. "What's the matter, Jeremy?" Jason asked, turning around to look at Jeremy.

"Nothing," Jeremy replied.

Instantly, Jason was on the bed beside his brother.

"I can help you," Jason offered quickly.

Jeremy smiled in spite of the difficult day he'd had. When Jason was born, Jeremy had been scared that his brother wasn't normal. At times he'd been jealous of the amount of attention Jason received. But Jason had an incredible ability to sense Jeremy's needs and try to meet them. His innocent and forgiving nature gave Jeremy a new perspective on the world.

As the oldest, Jeremy had felt responsible for caring for Jason. Jason had no concept of money or time and no preconceived ideas about people. But Jason was tenacious. When someone couldn't understand something he said, he refused to let that person go until he or she did understand. Jason would resort to spelling or searching his memory for a different word.

It wasn't that Jason hadn't had his moments, because he had. His sister, Kim, loved his big, blue bug-like eyes and the way Jason loved everyone around him. But the day Jason discovered the bright red fire alarm boxes after church, pulled the switches, and set off all the bells, had her squirming in red-faced embarrassment. "Mama, I could dig my own grave and bury myself," Kim fumed.

Ruth had nodded sympathetically. Her prayers had often been, "Lord, I'm up against a wall here"; "Lord, I'm discouraged"; or "Lord, I'm embarrassed. You gave me this child, and you are going to have to take me through this." She had come to realize that she must participate, not just sit back and pray without action. "God allowed it," she told a friend. "But I must accept my human responsibility. It is a great source of comfort because I know the Lord will take me through it."

Ruth insisted on a normal life, taking Jason everywhere they went—to basketball games, to rodeos, to the mall. She worked with him, teaching him to obey her rules.

Part of carrying on a normal life meant adjusting to changes in his siblings' relationships. When Kim decided to play basketball for the first time as an eighth grader, Ruth worried about the way Kim's new girlfriends and their families would relate to Jason. How accepting would they be?

After one game, everyone went to a local fast-food restaurant. The girls sat by themselves for a time, but then Jason wandered over to where they sat. "Oh, hi Jason," one of the girls said, making room for him at their table. As Jason talked with his new friends, an older boy came over and said something cruel. Like a group of mother hens, the girls surrounded Jason and walked him away from the tormentor. Ruth watched with warm approval.

One of Ruth's favorite verses was from Isaiah 55, "For as the heavens are higher than the earth, so are my ways higher than your ways." And she had found it to be so with her children.

Jeremy had begun working as an aide at a physical therapist's office and was thinking of studying physical therapy in college. "The patients love Jeremy," the therapist reported to Ruth one day. "He is patient and sensitive." Having the boys share a room had made a positive impact on both of them.

Stan admired the way Ruth had come to handle Jason—patiently and firmly. In the supermarket, when people began to stare at him when he tried to talk, she handled it by smiling at him and encouraging him. Her actions proclaimed, "This is my kid. I love him, and you can love him too."

Jason's supportive and affirming family life has made him willing to try new things, even though he may be scared at first. Jason may not win, and he may not always finish; but he will try. His trust and kindness may tempt others to take advantage of him. Both Ruth and Stan worry about the ugly parts of the world, parts that may intrude into Jason's world someday. But the compassion of new young friends brings them reassurance and hope.

"STAN, IT'S FOR YOU," RUTH SAID, giving Stan a quizzical look. The voice on the other end of the telephone line sounded familiar, but distorted by anxiety. Ruth realized that the caller was very upset.

"I'm coming right over," Stan said, then hung up.

"What's wrong?" Ruth asked with concern.

"JoJo was born with Down's," Stan said. "I'm going to run out and see them."

JoJo's parents were friends from seminary days. When Stan arrived, their faces told the story. Stan remembered the devastation he and Ruth had felt when Jason was born, their concerns about his condition and their abilities to raise him.

"She has Down's," JoJo's father repeated when Stan stepped inside.

"Yes, and you're going to love her anyway," Stan reassured the parents. "She's going to be a blast. You're going to learn things you'd never have learned otherwise."

"Like what?" they challenged him.

"Like unconditional love, the blessing of small advances, the meaning of true success."

STAN WAS NOT THE ONLY CARDER FAMILY MEMBER who used experiences with Jason to help others. Elaine, Ruth's sister, often had helped with Jason when they had lived nearby. Now she shared her knowledge with hurting couples in her husband's church. "I know you can make it, because we made it through a tough time when Jason was born." The greatest gift one can give to the mother of a baby is to love her child. Elaine had seen it happen in her own family. Jason was a wonderful human being, and she could say honestly that he had blessed the whole family.

Ruth was reaching out to others too. When a doctor told her of a woman in the church who had just had a baby with Down's syndrome, Ruth called the new mother right away.

"She's feeding the baby," the father said coldly.

"I won't interrupt her. My name is Ruth Carder. We have a son who was born with Down's syndrome. I just wanted to talk to her."

"Oh. Let me go get her," he said. Ruth recognized the instant rapport between people who have experienced similar circumstances. Suddenly the husband knew that Ruth would understand their emotional stress and anxiety.

When the mother came on the line, she said, "Mrs. Carder, all I really want is for someone to tell me it's going to be okay. Up to this point, I haven't had anyone tell me that this situation is going to be okay, that it's going to be something we can handle, that it is a child we can love. All I have heard is negative, negative, negative. I'm about to go nuts. I want to hear something positive."

Ruth smiled as she curled up on the couch. "Well, you're talking to the right woman. You have embarked upon a journey that's going to have many, many more ups than downs. Yes, you will have times of suffering, absolutely. But you are also going to have the most fun times. The things you take for granted with your other kids will become major milestones in the life of your Down's child. You will have a constant sense of ongoing anticipation and fulfillment."

As Ruth talked, she could hear the baby gurgle. Her heart went out to this family. She knew that if the parents didn't feel positive toward this child, they wouldn't find the positives; and the baby would sense this. Perhaps helping his parents see the positives could be her gift to this new little person.

Ruth's mind raced back to that bumpy flight to Salt Lake City and the caring people from the business community who had paid for Jason's flight. She remembered Elaine and Ted's coming to the hospital in Utah, Becky and Amy's regular visits to stimulate Jason. She recalled Jason in his little brown pants and white shirt doing somersaults on a horse, his racing up the hill out back with his dog. It's not like, gee, is this kid ever going to do anything? The answer is, this kid will do all kinds of things.

"Let me tell you what our son Jason is doing . . . " Lost in conversation, Ruth felt a warm little body snuggle close to her on the couch, his deep blue eyes sleepily reminding her that he was ready to be tucked in. "You're going to love that baby more than you can ever imagine," she promised.

EPILOGUE

Jason attends junior high school special education classes and will attend high school next year. He will continue in school until the age of twenty-one and then will work in a sheltered workshop. He enjoys sports, the Los Angeles Lakers, and the outdoors. Jeremy, a high school senior, works as a physical therapy aide and plans to attend college next year. Kim, a high school freshman, plays volleyball and basketball at school and enjoys playing the piano. Stan is pastor of special ministries at Grace Community Church, a church that serves 200 persons with disabilities through sports, camping, Sunday school class outings, worship services, and fellowship times. Ruth continues to be a mother at home and ministers to women who have children with disabilities. ❖

Bill

MOST WEEKENDS, ONE WOULD SEE THE LANKY YOUNG MAN patiently searching the beach for shells. Five little blonde daughters would race to grab his hand or to let him examine a sand-encrusted treasure. Bill Ryan had all the time in the world to listen, to watch, and to play with his family.

Invincible, June Ryan thought a few years later, tossing the volleyball back to her lively husband of twenty years.

"Okay, heads up, everybody!" Bill shouted over the blare of beach radios. "When it comes to you, just keep your eye on the ball and set it up to one of the girls on the front lines." The solid thud of the ball's being bandied back and forth by the older children with their accompanying shouts and squeals, confirmed that certain priorities—church, family, and work, in that order—had helped this family build a happy life. Bill believed in keeping the children busy, and he scheduled activities like this one every weekend.

As a teenager, her parents' hand holding and sitting close to each other in the car embarrassed Candy, but later she realized she was searching for a husband who possessed her dad's qualities. As Candy grew to adulthood, her father's devotion to her mother continued to amaze her. June managed a ladies' fashion shop. Bill, nearing retirement as manager of the Southern Bell Telephone Co. in south Florida, spent lunch hours, evenings, and Saturdays helping June at the shop.

As they reached retirement in 1978, they continued to be as active as ever. From 1982 to 1988 June and Bill worked together as volunteers in a West Palm Beach hospital. June's organizational skills kept her busy as president of the hospital auxiliary. Bill, an Irish tenor, entertained patients with Irish folk songs, ran errands, and comforted patients—all roles for which his friendly, outgoing personality and strong Christian values suited him. June and Bill were devout Catholics. They attended Mass daily, and Bill kept a rosary in his pocket as a lifelong habit.

JUNE PICKED UP THE PHONE IN HER OFFICE.

"June Ryan," she said.

"June, Bill's down here in the cafeteria. He's all upset. He says he can't find you," a volunteer alerted her.

"I've been in my office," June said, wondering why, after six years, Bill was having so much trouble finding his way around. "Tell him to stay there. I'll be right down." June was uneasy about Bill; his forgetfulness was making him defensive.

The combination of incidents over the past years convinced June that it was time for a neurologist to check Bill out. Bill agreed. The drive to the doctor's office only served to reinforce her suspicion that something was seriously wrong.

Recently Bill had had several near misses while driving, and she now had to help him be aware of traffic or obstacles. *Today getting to the doctor's office would be simple*, June thought. It was located at the hospital where they volunteered.

"You missed the exit," June said as they passed the ramp.

"I thought you said to go to the next exit," he covered.

Once inside, a nurse showed Bill to an examining room while June waited. It was an opportunity to speak to the doctor alone, and she seized it. In deciding whether it was time for Bill to surrender his driving privileges, she felt more comfortable enlisting the help of a trusted professional.

"Doctor, I'm afraid of Bill's driving," she said, describing Bill's confusion while behind the wheel.

"I'll tell Bill if I think he shouldn't drive," the doctor agreed. June followed him into the examining room.

"What did you think of the story of the stewardess who was thrown from an airplane in today's newspaper?" the doctor asked.

"I didn't read the paper," Bill replied, although he had.

The doctor continued to question Bill during the examination.

"Listen Bill," the doctor said casually. "I've just moved here from New York. West Palm is one of the worst places I've seen for traffic. I think you ought to stop driving."

Bill said nothing.

"Bill, you can go ahead and get dressed. Mrs. Ryan, let's step into the hall."

"What do you think?" June asked as the door closed.

"Short-term memory loss. Let's schedule some tests to be certain nothing else is going on."

In the hospital lobby, Bill dropped the car keys into June's hand. "Okay, sweetheart, it's all yours," he said, and June drove from then on.

BILL UNDERWENT AN MRI TEST, but it did not indicate Alzheimer's disease. June was sixty-nine and Bill was seventy, and they agreed it was time to sell the house in West Palm Beach. They moved to a Tallahassee apartment complex just five minutes from their daughters Diann and Elyse. With Joy in San Antonio, Texas; Candy ten hours away near Miami, Florida; and Denise in Memphis, Tennessee, it was a comfort to be near two of their children. Once settled in, they got together regularly to visit and to watch the grandkids grow up.

June had looked forward to spending an evening at Elyse's house. As they arrived, Elyse was waiting at the front door. "Daddy, Mother, I'm so glad you're here," she said, hugging her father. As Elyse prepared the dining room, setting her fine china on a pressed white tablecloth, June chatted happily with her son-in-law, Jim. *How happy they are*, June thought, enjoying the moment.

Bill's angry voice broke in, "We're going. Good-bye, Elyse."

"Darling, we haven't eaten yet. Other people are coming; we just can't go now," June said gently.

Elyse was bewildered. "Daddy, please . . . "

Bill's look as he brushed past their youngest daughter shocked June. His actions were so unlike him, but the look—as if Elyse were a complete stranger and he was trying to figure out who she was—baffled her. Once outside, Bill fiddled with the car door, got it open, and slid into the passenger seat where he sat defiantly with his arms crossed. Shocked and confused, June promised Elyse she'd call later, apologized again, then drove Bill home in silence.

Once inside the apartment, Bill marched down the hallway to their bedroom and sat on the bed staring at the television without turning it on. June came into the room and sat beside him on the bed.

"Darlin' we've got to see somebody about my mind," he said plaintively. "I'm not in my right mind. Something is happening to me."

"I'll schedule an appointment at the Mayo Clinic as quickly as possible," June promised.

ON AUGUST 6, 1991, WHICH WAS BILL'S BIRTHDAY, June and Bill drove to the Mayo Clinic in Jacksonville. Follow-up tests with a clinic psychiatrist after their initial visit, this time with Elyse along, confirmed a diagnosis of Alzheimer's disease (AD). "He only gets about one-half of what we say," the psychiatrist said. He then warned her that any type of surgery could escalate the disease and should be avoided.

June stared at the doctor. The diagnosis of Alzheimer's meant that Bill would lose his mind and eventually die. With strong commitment, June resolved that Bill would have as full and as happy a life as she could provide.

Literature from the Alzheimer's Association explained, "(AD) is a progressive, degenerative disease that attacks the brain and results in impaired memory, thinking and behavior. It is the most common form of demential illness. The person with AD may experience confusion, personality and behavior changes, impaired judgment, and difficulty finding words, finishing thoughts or following directions."

For the past ten years, June had told their daughters when they tried to talk to her about their dad, "He's just getting older." Reading the information provided by the Alzheimer's Association made June realize that Bill's forgetfulness was not age-associated memory impairment. Memory impairment meant that persons forgot parts of experiences but remembered them later. Bill simply forgot the experience and did not remember it.

Bill and June's daughter, Diann, was a trainer for the school district. She could see that her mom was exhausted and trying to get organized, while her dad became increasingly confused. With the Alzheimer's diagnosis, they now had a starting point for gathering helpful information. Both Elyse and Diann offered to accompany their mom to support group meetings specifically for Alzheimer's care-givers.

While Diann attended an Alzheimer's caregiver support group with their mom, Elyse stayed with their dad and vice versa. The support group met many needs. It provided hints like cleaning out closets and drawers of unnecessary clothing to make choices less confusing, removing furniture and throw rugs that can cause persons to trip. Both June and the girls heard other caregivers describe behaviors that Bill also had: outbursts over minor frustration, asking for the same information over and over.

In just one month, doctors had diagnosed Bill with a terminal illness, and nothing in modern medical science could change it. He would never be well again. Just facing that fact brought a heartache that those who have not walked that road could not understand. The support group members listened and didn't press them to hurry through their telling of the struggle. Those in the group the longest gave testimony that you could hang on and keep your loved one at home. June believed that if she just took good care of Bill, he would get well. When he didn't, she blamed herself.

Bill was furious when June and Diann returned to Elyse's house after the meeting. "Why did you leave me? Take me home now!" he shouted, the veins standing out on his neck.

After they left, Diann said to Elyse, "I'm sure she's in for a horrible experience when she gets home. He thinks he's been abandoned." Diann had learned at the support meeting that some outbursts are triggered because people with Alzheimer's don't know where they have been or where they are going, and they are so very frightened. It was clear that their mother was losing the loving support of their father. They would need to demonstrate their love for their mom more than ever.

Within a few days, Elyse offered to spend the night at her parents' apartment so her mother could get some rest. Incredibly, her father did not sleep at all that night. "Where have all the people gone?" he asked over and over. Bill got up seventeen times to see where June was. "She's asleep on the couch," Elyse told him, walking with him down the hall so he could see for himself, then back to his room. Once back in bed and covered with a sheet, he fretted because he could only remember part of his evening prayers. "Where's your mother?" he wondered aloud, climbing back out of bed. Elyse walked him to the living room again.

TEARS RAN DOWN JUNE'S CHEEKS AS SHE TELEPHONED Bill's doctor at the Mayo Clinic. He had forewarned her to avoid any surgery for Bill but now that seemed unavoidable. Bill's Tallahassee physician had just explained that a complete exam clearly revealed the need for emergency prostate surgery. The words of Bill's doctor at Mayo Clinic filled June with dread: "June, you'll have to keep a stiff upper lip. After surgery Bill could be very violent and agitated. You're going to require help. He'll need twenty-four hour supervision."

The behaviors cited by Alzheimer's support group members started as soon as Bill was out of surgery. He didn't recognize his wife or children. He couldn't feed himself or control his bowels or bladder. To add some cheeriness to the room, Elyse strung up a brightly colored banner that sent him into shrieks of terror until she pulled it down and hid it. Frightened and combative, Bill rarely calmed down. Medications had little or no effect in controlling his irrational fear. The ones that did work only worked for a couple of days. For the three and one-half weeks that Bill was a patient, two of the three women (June, Diann, and Elyse) were at his side around the clock, catching catnaps on a cot in his room.

June could count on visits from their parish priests. During Bill's hospital stay, they alternated visits each night. As the priest sat by Bill's bed, reciting the age-old rosary consisting of the Hail Mary and Our Father prayers plus the five mysteries of the faith and the Stations of the Cross, she felt the strength of her religion helping her endure. FATHER MICHAEL and FATHER ROGER's faithful visits strengthened her for the uncertain future. Others from Good Shepherd Catholic Church stopped by to visit at the hospital and sent flowers as a reminder of their care.

Some well-meaning persons suggested, "Put him in a nursing home, if they'll keep him." For June, that was not an option. Elyse and Diann discussed caregiving with their spouses. Elyse's husband traveled; but the nights he was home, she would spend the night to care for her father. Diann could stay part of the weekend. Thus, the family decided to bring Bill home.

As Jim, Elyse's husband, turned into the wooded apartment complex of gray buildings with neatly trimmed landscaping, June relaxed a little. She assured herself that the strange hospital surroundings had caused Bill's bizarre behavior and that the familiar surroundings of home would soothe him.

"Here we are, home at last, Bill," she said, leading him in their door. Here were familiar things—the beige-carpeted living room; the "Florida" couch with its bright floral pinks, greens, and yellows; the white easy chair and footstool with the nubby fabric.

"Would you like to go into your bedroom or stay here?" June asked.

Bill looked straight at June and wordlessly sat down in the white chair he'd always hated. June had lunch ready and heated a pot of tea, Bill's favorite, as she set out plates and napkins. She allowed the tea to cool to lukewarm so Bill wouldn't scald himself, then suggested, "Let's go into the table." She helped Bill to his seat. When he had finished eating, he dumped the uneaten half of his sandwich into his tea. June asked, "Do you want me to make more tea?"

Bill clenched his large hand into a tight fist and shook it at his wife. The gentle, kind man with the Phil Donahue hair, who wore Izod shirts and khaki trousers and had a deep, wonderful laugh, had become a Dr. Jekyll in diapers, loose pajama pants, and an oversized flannel shirt.

As the girls scrapped their plan to bring the grandchildren over later, June felt pricked by another loss. Isolating Bill from the grandkids meant that she would not see them either.

That first day Bill stood up and sat down repeatedly. June stood up with him each time, holding his arm so he wouldn't topple over. The family members had known they would need some help. Elyse had picked up literature about Alzheimer's at the hospital and sent it out to other family members to orient them to the struggle that lay ahead.

June had much to learn. At one time, she had looked forward to nightfall and bedtime as a time of quiet, dark, and rest. Now as the sun went down and she tried to prepare Bill for bed, she found herself badly frightened as he flailed out, becoming more and more agitated. Everything in the apartment bothered him. He jumped when he saw his reflection in mirrors, so she took them down and closed the door to the bathroom with its full mirror. She packed up the pictures on the walls and on table tops. Glassware, knickknacks, and throw rugs disappeared. June covered the furniture with sheets, and the apartment took on a plain, antiseptic quality.

Since too much information confused Bill, June learned to talk in short sentences. She kept Bill out of the kitchen when she cooked lest he touch a hot burner, and she quickly discovered that Bill would attempt to eat a houseplant or a tablecloth as readily as a sandwich.

By the second day of Bill's return home, they agreed it was time for professional help. June hired an agency aide to come from 11 P.M. and stay until 6 A.M. on weeknights. During this time, Bill was likely to be roaming the apartment screaming. Like a child, he saw June jump to his yells, so he yelled louder. She turned on all the fans in the apartment to muffle the noise, but she worried that the neighbors would complain.

When a call to Bill's surgeon about his extreme fright at night produced no suggestions, Diann passed along to her mother a reference book, *The 36-Hour Day*. June read about Sundown Syndrome, a reaction to darkness that causes some Alzheimer's patients to become agitated. That same day, Elyse came to watch Bill while June purchased a half dozen lamps.

When the sun set, June turned on all the lamps in the house. That night, with bright lights on, and the fan blowing over his bed all night, Bill was calm. He slept two hours instead of waking every forty-five minutes.

Within months, the family agreed that the aide was too expensive, and Diann and Elyse began to stay overnight. A second attempt to employ an aide ended when the young man failed to arrive regularly. The family agreed that they themselves would provide the level of care Bill needed and deserved.

To watch her beloved husband—an intellectual person who was fun to be with—lose his mind before his physical body gave way was not only difficult for June. She knew it was difficult for him too. Sometimes during a quiet moment, when she brushed his hair or shaved him, Bill's beautiful blue eyes would crinkle up and a fleeting smile would pull at his mouth. As he whispered, "Thank you, darlin'," she knew that he knew.

DIANN WAS GLAD THE FAMILY MEMBERS HAD AGREED to keep her father at home, but the task was overwhelming. Diann's strongest supporter was a friend whose father had suffered a stroke. This friend had spent four months with her father on the midnight to 6 A.M. shift in the hospital. She understood the emotional upheaval, fear, and exhaustion that constant care and worry bring. They commiserated about the strain of staying up all night to help with their fathers and the difficulty of concentrating on work after a sleepless night.

When Diann explained their circumstances to her neighbor, the woman said, "I didn't know it was like this." She offered to keep Diann's little girl whenever Diann needed to be with her father. Realizing that the woman was sincere, Diann did not hesitate to call and accept her offer. As other neighbors learned of the situation, they also offered to help with child care.

At the office, Diann realized she had bad days when her father had bad days. Coworkers were warm and understanding. They were as compassionate the first time she said, "This is a bad day; I don't think he'll last another day," as the twentieth time.

When Elyse got her children off to preschool, she would go to her parents' apartment to give her mother a break. On those weekdays when the kids were out of school, Elyse came in her van with the kids. When she tooted her horn, June would run out and jump in, while Elyse ran into the apartment. June then could spend a few precious hours doting on her grandkids and attending 9 A.M. Mass with the children at a small chapel.

EVEN IF THEY ARRIVED FOR THE LAST FIVE MINUTES OF MASS, church friends would save a place for June and her grandchildren. This small group of daily Mass goers had welcomed June and Bill warmly when a year and a half earlier they had moved to Tallahassee. They often went to a fast food restaurant after church for fellowship. Bill and June had felt at home with this group from their first meeting. The children loved to go with their grandmother for hamburgers and fries with the group. The outings were therapeutic for everyone. June got a break and an opportunity to share the love and vigor of her grandchildren with her friends. They doted on the children too; and when it was time to go home, the children didn't want to leave.

One day Diann received a call from a woman in the group, "I know your mom has you and your sister, but I think she also needs people her own age. We want to take her out to dinner. Will you stay with your dad next Tuesday?" Diann was thrilled. She knew the older women could give her mother a different kind of support. They might encourage her mother to confide her fears and could offer a new perspective.

Along with the 9 A.M. Mass group, the parish priests continued to be available to the family. One night, Father Roger came to call at 10 P.M.; June had asked him to come and pray with Bill. As the priest recited the prayers Bill had learned as a little boy, June watched Bill begin to relax. The prayers comforted her too, reminding her of the faith that had helped her in other struggles. To her, it was like giving her burdens to someone who is more knowledgeable and experienced. As the priest continued the prayers, June slipped out of the room. She could get a load of laundry done and wash a few dishes while he sat with Bill. When she had finished her chores in the kitchen, she slipped back into Bill's room.

"June, I'll come earlier next time," Father Roger told her. "But instead of working, I want you to promise to go out and take a walk or visit a neighbor while I'm here. You need a break too, and you're not getting it by working every time someone comes."

AS JUNE AND HER DAUGHTERS MAINTAINED an around-the-clock vigil with Bill, the Alzheimer's book title *The 36-Hour Day* made perfect sense. An exhausting night replaced a day of challenges, and another day followed the night.

June mentally ticked off the stops she could fit in the two hours that Elyse would stay that morning. Before Bill's surgery, the residents of the apartment complex had been used to seeing the couple leaving each morning for Mass. A young woman they'd befriended at the pool that summer noticed Bill's absence and asked if something were wrong.

June was pleased that DEBBIE, a casual acquaintance, had noticed and cared enough to inquire. Debbie offered to sit with Bill several times so June could get out, but June put her off each time.

"June . . ."

"Oh, hi," June said, rolling down the car window. She'd been so distracted that she failed to see Debbie's purposeful approach. June could tell Debbie wanted to say something as she stood by the car holding her seven-year-old daughter's hand. Bill's "Little Jimmy" adventure stories that ended with a moral had enchanted the little girl by the poolside.

"You know I've offered to come sit with Bill so many times. You always say, 'That's okay, Diann is coming' or 'Elyse is coming.' I had a son with cerebral palsy that I cared for at home for a number of years. Many well-meaning people said to me, 'Call me.' One morning I had an emergency with Eric. I was frantic until I remembered all the people who had offered to help. I called, but they all had shopping dates. When my son died, I made up my mind that if I ever offer to help, I will be there."

Debbie's words stunned June. She hadn't accepted Debbie's offer because she didn't want to impose. Accepting Debbie's offer for even fifteen minutes would allow her to get a shower. Bill became so distraught that he screamed when she showered or ran the half block to the mailbox. Debbie's offer to come could meet both their needs.

Debbie's revealing to June her deepest wound acted as a healing agent to both women. June reversed her decision not to "bother" Debbie as she realized that this calm, friendly young woman's loss of a son had created a need in her to share her gifts of care and compassion. This revelation was the key that unlocked June's ability to receive, and even to ask for, help from friends and paid professionals.

The next day June called Debbie and invited her to come. "I'll only be gone an hour," she said, pleased that Debbie sounded grateful for being asked. When Debbie arrived, she spoke in a quiet, high-pitched voice that seemed to please Bill. June saw that Bill remembered her and appeared comfortable. Debbie moved slowly and deliberately, giving him time to get used to her.

June explained Bill's routine and what to expect, leaving several emergency numbers. Debbie became a willing helper, and it was hard to tell who got more out of her visits—Debbie or Bill.

"You know, you will never have any guilt feelings when he dies," Debbie told June one afternoon.

Debbie's words brought unexpected comfort. She was someone who had experienced the death of a beloved child, had made decisions that paralleled June's, and in retrospect was at peace with her choices. All of these positives gave June new courage.

"THINGS ARE GETTING HAIRY," ELYSE CONFIDED, when her sister JOY made one of her weekly telephone calls from Texas. Joy wanted to fly down immediately to help, but she knew that was unrealistic. Her husband's career in the Air Force kept him away. As the parents of three children, Joy and her husband Gregory, knew they couldn't dash off to Florida each time a crisis arose. Joy had even had to wait until her husband returned from an assignment to come after her dad's emergency surgery.

DENISE, with a nine-year-old son, combined marriage and career. She called often from Tennessee, speaking almost daily to her mother. She too felt burdened by the guilt of not being there to help. "Mom, I'm coming down next week," she said. "I can at least take the night shift for a few days and give you a break."

As each daughter spent time giving care, they developed an understanding of the complex needs and emotions Alzheimer's creates. Whenever one of the out-of-town sisters got a call requesting help, she went. As the months passed, the family hired agency nurses to check on Bill. The nurses checked him for bedsores, and they could administer an enema for constipation when necessary. But at $25.00 an hour, the family needed to use nursing services sparingly. The family also hired the services of a home health care agency that provided nurses' aides five days a week to change the diaper Bill wore, bathe him, and take his temperature.

Elyse continued to come by the apartment faithfully, and easily identified with the strain on her mother, who was now seventy-one. Finding affordable, caring aides added to June's anxiety. Several times their mother had witnessed rough treatment by a paid aide.

AFTER SUNDAY MASS, June stayed for a few minutes to talk with friends. "There is a wonderful man who volunteers his time with Alzheimer's patients," a woman told her. "Here's his number. You won't be disappointed." Finally June called, setting a time for an initial visit when Elyse could be with them.

How cute, she thought, when WILL arrived. A big, burly Irishman in his sixties, he wore a bright emerald green cap and cable-knit, green wool Irish sweater.

"I'm Will," he said with an assurance that came from meeting strangers hundreds of times a week as a former New York cop. As Will sat down on the sofa next to Elyse, Bill watched from his chair, and smiled.

Will shared a little of his background. The women learned that he'd been in the novice program for the priesthood and had been a member of the Third Order of St. Francis for fifty-four years. He had been a commander of the American Legion; and after retirement, joined a Retired Senior Volunteer Program (RSVP). He knew it was normal for the family of an Alzheimer's patient to be apprehensive about having someone new come to help with a loved one.

"I sat with a fellow named Frank. He put pots and pans in the bathtub," Will told June and Elyse. "I was once a golden gloves boxer, and I could see him get tense when people tried to stop his harmless activities. I think it's best to leave persons with Alzheimer's alone if what they are doing isn't harmful."

Turning to June, Will asked, "Was Bill a serviceman? What did he like to do?" June appreciated his asking about Bill. Bill's life had been wonderful, and it gave her pleasure to share it with Will. June told Will of Bill's Irish ancestry and his military service. As they talked, they realized they had a lot in common: they were all Catholic, had come from New York, were retired; and the two men shared an ethnic heritage. Will, seeing that Bill was relaxed, moved over to the white nubby footstool near him. "Hi, buddy," he said. "We old soldiers have to stick together, don't we?"

As Will continued to talk, June and Elyse slipped into the bedroom. Will's caring presence had given them hope. "I think he's a winner," Elyse said, hugging her mother.

Will came each evening from 4:30 to 8:30. He had that rare ability to make everyone feel better. He delighted the family with quotes from Shakespeare and tales of New York police work. To Will, June was Mrs. Ryan, and Bill was Billy.

It seemed to June that God had said, "Here, I am sending Bill a male friend." The whole family felt that Will's masculine influence helped a part of their dad that needed to relate to a man.

June drew both physical and emotional strength from Will's nightly visits. As she cleared away coffee cups and rinsed them in the sink, Will's deep voice drifted back to her and she smiled. He was singing "My Sweet Molly Malone," an Irish folk song that Bill had sung so many times to patients in West Palm Beach. Will would get Bill ready for bed—put his loose pajamas on him, place a clean disposable pad on the bed in the stark, brightly lit bedroom. His efforts saved her strength for the long night ahead when she would struggle to get Bill out of his sweat-soaked pajamas three or four times, gently smooth his hair and talk with him to calm him, change the sheets, and try to close her eyes for a few minutes.

June dried her hands and walked down the brightly lit hall to peek in on the two men, Will singing and Bill restlessly nodding his head to the words. When he finished the song, Will conjured up visions of Ireland, "Billy, think of the River Shannon, how it gently flows down to the sea with the sun on its banks. We feel relaxed and we want to sleep."

HELPING GAVE WILL A GOOD FEELING. It was a type of outreach that made sense to him based on his own Bible study. A lot of cops he knew, himself included, could be harsh one minute dealing with a criminal; and tender and compassionate the next, helping an injured person. Here at last was an opportunity to do work in which he didn't have to hurt anyone. Here was something that made him feel good at the end of the day when he sat in his backyard and looked at the statue of Saint Francis in his flower garden.

RITA MOSS moved to Tallahassee and promptly inquired at her new church for opportunities to give respite care. She had been a member of the National Catholic Council of Women prior to moving and had given respite care through them. When she learned that Good Shepherd Catholic Church had no such group, the retired homemaker asked for volunteers to start one. She invited a geriatric nurse and a psychologist to speak to interested volunteers about quality caregiving issues. Rita then announced through notices to senior citizens' groups and two hospitals that the group offered respite care. She also placed the information in the weekly Sunday bulletin. Some of the volunteers had limited hours to offer. Others did not want to sit with terminal patients, and Rita honored their requests.

Rita had lots of free time, and she felt that she got more out of helping than she gave. Her uncle, who lived some distance away, had Parkinson's disease. She wished someone would offer respite to her aunt, but no one did.

June saw the notice in the church bulletin and called Rita, who suggested that she come out and get acquainted first. "Bill, this is our new friend, Rita," June told her husband when Rita arrived. He held out his hand in greeting. "Hello Bill," Rita said, treating him as she would anyone else. "I brought some roses for you to enjoy."

Bill rewarded Rita with a huge smile as the sweet aroma of the half-dozen roses perfumed the room. Bill had always loved caring for flowers.

Rita and June talked for a half hour, and June began to feel that here was a friend. Rita was retired, stable, and dependable. She came with an attitude of doing the best she could, an attitude that seemed to keep her from becoming overwhelmed with the situation.

June was honest with Rita, "I might be hesitant to have someone come in and care for Bill," she said. In the back of her mind, she worried that Bill could fall and break a hip, or fall and injure a volunteer. A world of difference separated being ill and having dementia. June and Rita resolved those issues.

When Rita had arrived, June thought Rita's small size might prevent her from being able to handle Bill. But when Bill tried to get up, Rita firmly took him by the shoulder and helped him to sit down again. The deft way she handled Bill gave June additional evidence that Rita could cope with Bill.

"Bill, June is going to get groceries when I come back on Thursday," Rita said as she rose to leave. The two women agreed on a time, and June had every confidence Rita would be there.

June found herself confiding in Rita on the telephone. Rita, over the years, had learned to be patient and compassionate with people. Her feeling was, you don't turn your back when people need you. When she learned that Bill and June had attended 9 A.M. Mass, she arranged her schedule to be certain June could attend the whole service on the days she sat with Bill.

Rita stayed with Bill two or three times each week for about two hours at a time. Bill was the first person with Alzheimer's disease that Rita had spent time with. Soon she came to understand the need for a break. When Bill became agitated the least bit, he'd groan, "Oh mnd mnd mnd mnd mnd mnd . . . " over and over. Rita could say to herself, *In a couple of hours, I will leave; I can handle this.*

When Rita first came to relieve June, Bill did not sit still. She spent her time holding his arm to keep him from falling. Later she sat and talked to Bill about old times or sang hymns. Rita always carried her rosary beads. It pleased June that Rita shared her faith with them.

"Bill, I'd like to say the rosary with you," she'd say, pulling out her beads. For June, it was a peaceful time as Rita prayed with Bill.

Rita's ability to provide appropriate care freed June to run needed errands, or to slip into the other bedroom for a nap.

ALTHOUGH JUNE FOUND IT DIFFICULT TO ALLOW OTHERS TO CARE for Bill, her positive experiences with Will, Rita, and Debbie gave her the courage to call on the St. Paul's United Methodist Church Alzheimer's Respite Ministry. She believed that church volunteers would be kind—if only Bill qualified.

A study of community needs had showed that respite care was the number one need in the city. This church created a careful, deliberate plan with a specific model to provide a respite ministry.

Alzheimer's disease complicates issues in the areas of death, dying, and loss. Persons must work through complex emotions as the patient's personality dies, followed by physical death. Training as a respite caregiver is vital. Through training, volunteers increase their awareness of these issues, which enables them to be more nurturing. Training also includes safety tips and basic first aid.

"This disease can last for years," the director tells her volunteers. "Consider the loss of sleep, the stress as both Alzheimer's patient and spouse or caretaker become house bound; the financial devastation as the wage earner quits his or her job to become a caregiver or pays for nursing care. Consider the cost of medications, diapers, linen service. This all adds up to an incredible emotional strain and drain. And the well family member is powerless to stop the process."

The training and support group meetings make use of guest speakers, including a physician who discusses normal aging and Alzheimer's. The medical information helps to demystify and explain the disease. A video available through the Alzheimer's Association, "Living with Grace," gives trainees a vivid picture of Alzheimer's by following an Alzheimer's patient.

MARGARET HOOPER DETERMANN became the director of the St. Paul's Alzheimer's respite program in April 1992. She recognized the need for a support group for caregivers that allowed them to share what went on at home. "No one really understands unless they've been there," she explained the day June came to listen. "Here is a place that you can come when your family and friends don't understand why you keep talking about it—a place to go to talk about the daily struggle to give a loved one a bath or the unpredictability of this disease. You'll find that having somebody nod their head because they have been there too will give you comfort and strength for the days ahead."

At these meetings, June found support, understanding, and valuable tips. She could be brutally honest and express anger, frustration, or whatever she was feeling without having to justify her feelings. At home she could no longer laugh or tease with Bill—those behaviors now intimidated him. Here people understood her feelings and weren't shocked by what she had to share.

ABOUT HALF OF THE VOLUNTEERS HAD AN ASSOCIATION with illness and wanted to help other people. The respite volunteers did not act as nurses or aides and did not do hands-on caring, such as bathing or moving clients. They acted more as companions: feeding, visiting, looking through books, taking walks, watching television, or listening to music with the Alzheimer's client. They learned to keep their voices clear and calm, to speak and to move slowly, to state their intentions clearly using the patients' names, and to be prepared to answer the same question over and over.

Bill had lost the purposeful use of his hands, which made some activities that occupied Alzheimer's patients such as coloring, paint by numbers, and sorting, impossible. Bill liked tactile things and became attached to an old doll June had made, keeping it on his lap much of the time.

Volunteers and clients at St. Paul's came in a variety of ages and backgrounds. The center would call on them over the next six months to give June respite. None of them knew June or Bill, but each had a need to care for others.

MARY MAUD SHARPE was a recent retiree and teacher of two year olds at the church. She decided to take the training.

RUTH KELLOGG was a people person and had worked as a social worker for twenty-three years before her retirement three years earlier. She felt that anything a family could do to keep a loved one at home was important. She had raised eight children and knew what it was like to be a caregiver and have to spread yourself thin.

JANICE NASH, a kindergarten teacher, looked for some new ministry to help with every few years. She felt that respite care was the right thing for her to do in the summer. She took the training, which gave her the security of knowing what types of behavior she might face.

Talking over a plan to provide respite care for June, Margaret reassured her, "The best way to keep taking care of him, is to take care of you." Her words helped June feel okay about taking time off for herself. Margaret had been impressed by June's ability to accept help and saw her as a role model for other caregivers. This woman was doing a great many things right—staying connected with her church, getting exercise to relieve stress, and allowing others to help—and it showed.

WHEN JUNE CALLED ST. PAUL'S, Margaret assigned Mary Maud to relieve June for a few hours. Mary Maud's calming presence impressed June immediately. A small woman in her late sixties, Mary Maud came right in as if she had known Bill for years. Bill liked Mary Maud too and called her "Rose Lady." When they first met, Bill could still communicate, using a few words.

"Bill, this is Mary Maud," June said.

"I made you some cookies Bill," Mary Maud said. "And I brought you some roses. I'll put them on this table."

Once June saw that Mary Maud and Bill were comfortable with each other, the two women agreed Mary Maud would arrive each Wednesday from 9 A.M. and stay until after lunch. During that time June could go to Mass, accept a luncheon engagement, or just sleep in her own bedroom. Mary Maud would look at picture books from the forties and fifties with Bill or listen to music from that era.

As the months passed, Mary Maud's admiration for June's strength and courage and her ability to know when it was time to get away grew. When Elyse suggested that her mother go to the coast for a few days, June turned to Mary Maud.

"I hate to go, but my girls say I need a rest," June said.

"Yes, June. It would probably do you good," Mary Maud agreed. "Count on me to stay longer on the days you are gone."

Mary Maud had told Margaret Determann earlier, "Sometimes I think, *I just don't have time to go this week.* But when I get there, I know that I do have the time. The families are so grateful and so nice. When they say, 'I can't pay you back,' I tell them that sooner or later they'll pass it on."

Ruth Kellogg sat with Bill two times a week. She also placed her name on call for the times when June was ill. Her care allowed June to rest and recuperate. While sitting with Bill, she fed him, administered medication, and held his hand. Bill liked to have someone nearby, and he found physical touch reassuring.

THE ST. PAUL'S ALZHEIMER'S GROUP INSTRUCTIONS prepared Janice Nash to meet with June when she called for respite. The elementary school where Janice taught had just closed for summer vacation. Janice had activated her name on the Alzheimer's respite list for the summer months. Janice felt that respite care was something she could do, although she was somewhat afraid of the disease and of what she might encounter. She trusted in her own abilities and took the leap of faith that is so necessary for growth—she stepped out and tried it. She found that caring for Bill Ryan was not that difficult.

When they first met, Janice noticed how tired June looked. The kind way in which June included Bill in their conversation, patted him on the shoulder, or smoothed his hair as he became agitated, all spoke of June's strong love for her husband. She felt honored that June would consider allowing her to care for Bill. Janice felt the depth of trust that June placed in her.

Janice was drawn to Bill even though she could never know his true personality. Paging through old photo albums, she commented to June, "You can just see the love in his eyes," which gave June an opportunity to reflect on Bill's beautiful way of relating to his family that had been lost to the disease.

"He is still a really sweet man," Janice reassured June. "I want to know him and all his wonderful stories." Soon Janice and June were sharing information about their families and growing closer. As Janice talked about her own family with its normal problems, joys, and accomplishments, she lifted June's spirits.

Janice had been born and raised in The United Methodist Church. "Doing unto others" was an important part of her life. Her father had passed away and her elderly mother lived some distance away. It wasn't hard to put herself in the Ryans' shoes. She hoped that if the time ever came, someone would help her.

At 11:30 Janice checked her watch. June would not return for another hour that day. "Bill, I am going to take you to the kitchen table for some lunch," she said, letting him know what she was doing as she took his elbow. Bill's bright blue eyes followed her hand as she spoon-fed him pureed turkey that June had prepared. It had the consistency of baby food, but his mouth didn't seem to work right. Finally Bill simply closed his mouth and refused to take another bite.

Janice laughed to herself. *Now what do I do?* she wondered. Finally she got up, filled a glass of water at the kitchen sink, and held it out to Bill. Without hesitating he reached for the glass, "Thank you," he said. Janice felt a tremble go through her as she stared at Bill. He had not spoken to her for two months. For a fleeting second he had crossed that bridge back into her world, and she was overcome with a wave of tenderness. The effect on her was impossible to explain to people who had not lost a loved one to dementia—but the Ryan family understood.

As the summer came to an end, Janice prepared to return to teaching and removed her name from the active respite group list. She was glad she had acted on her urge to try something new. It made her feel good to give June a little free time, and she found herself thinking of the Ryans often as she prepared her classroom for the coming year.

As she drove home from school one afternoon, Janice glanced at her watch. She could be at June's house in just a couple of minutes, but she only had a half hour to give. As she dropped a quarter in a pay phone, she wondered if she were being silly.

"I know the doctor has told you to get out and get some exercise for your health. I've got thirty minutes and wondered if you'd like me to stop by so you can get in a quick swim?"

"Oh Janice, that's so nice of you—but it's not necessary," June replied, then stopped. "Yes, I'd love to. I'll be ready when you get here." When Janice arrived minutes later, June was in her swimsuit with a terry cover-up over it and a brightly colored beach towel in hand. "Thanks," she said as they passed.

The cool water, combined with fifteen minutes of lap swimming, was invigorating. When she climbed out of the pool, June still had time for conversation with friends who were at the pool. With renewed enthusiasm for the rest of the day, June called good-bye and headed home to relieve Janice.

BILL HAD BEEN AT HOME FOR SEVEN MONTHS when Elyse approached her mother with a suggestion for celebrating her parents' golden wedding anniversary. "We had always planned to give you and dad a big celebration," Elyse told her mother. "We'd still like to celebrate. It could be quiet and nice—and fun."

The girls knew their mother had looked forward to celebrating the milestone, and they wanted to honor their parents in some special way. June had often said, "When our fiftieth comes, we'll celebrate and all be together." They all knew the end would come sooner than they had hoped. This celebration would be a way to affirm their love for one another.

Anticipating the wedding anniversary and making plans gave everyone a boost. All of the sisters flew in to be with their mother and father and attend a special 9 A.M. Mass in honor of Bill and June's fifty years of marriage while a respite volunteer stayed with Bill for the day. The priests wore white vestments signifying a celebration and friends made a banner with golden letters that said, "Happy Golden Anniversary, Bill and June." A special poem from DOROTHY and EMIL, friends who had welcomed Bill and June to the church and entertained them at their country club, reminded June that others recognized the joy and the pain that wrapped itself around her that day.

After the Mass, Elyse and Jim hosted a luncheon at their home. As friends gathered around, Candy, Joy, Denise, Diann, and Elyse surrounded their mother and presented her with a gift. "This is from Daddy and us," they said. "Happy golden anniversary." Carefully June lifted the lid of the box. She slipped the wedding band with six diamonds—one for each of the children and one for Bill—on her finger. Simply being together, renewed the sisters' strength.

As preparations got underway for the anniversary, a reporter with the Florida public radio network contacted June and invited her to speak on the radio about Alzheimer's disease. It would air as a special feature about Alzheimer's stories. The reporter came to visit June, and she followed her usual habit of introducing everyone who entered the apartment as she took the reporter back to Bill's bedroom. "These people want to talk to me about our life," she said, and the visitors stood in the doorway and smiled. "They're friends of ours." Bill looked from one friendly face to the next and smiled.

The opportunity to share her experience put June in a role with which she was familiar—that of volunteering her time to help other people. She hoped her sharing would convince others of the value of respite care.

BY THE END OF SUMMER BILL WEIGHED SEVENTY-EIGHT POUNDS and was confined to his bed. June feared that Bill had pneumonia, but she could not convince a doctor to come and examine him. The doctor explained that due to insurance regulations, he could not come. June would have to bring Bill to his office. June called an ambulance to arrange the trip, but a pounding rainstorm changed her mind. She had seen a young doctor at church that morning but did not think to call him. Later the doctor's wife called Elyse.

"How is your dad doing?" she asked.

"I don't know," Elyse answered. "The nurse says Daddy is dying, but we don't know for certain if the end is near," she confided. "No doctor will come to check on him."

Within an hour the young doctor had come to talk to June and then to see Bill. "It will be between two and three weeks. His breathing signals that the end is near; his lungs are full."

Suddenly June was frightened. "Should we go to the hospital?"

"For what? Another week of agony?" the doctor asked kindly. "It looks like God is telling us that this is Bill's time, and I am certain he is more comfortable here than he would be in a hospital."

Before he left, the doctor promised to send his nurse the next day. Though the nurse came to check on Bill daily, June never received a bill.

Father Roger and Father Michael came to administer the sacrament of extreme unction (anointing the sick) and remained faithful in their visitation. Will arrived daily—talking, singing, and working to feed Bill. Rita came to sit by Bill's bed, to hold his hand, and to say rosaries.

The daughters came to be with their father; but as he seemed to weather his crisis, they returned home. Ten days later, on Tuesday, September 1, 1992, Bill died at home. June, Elyse, Diann, and Candy had been at his side all day, praying and singing his beloved Irish folk songs. A sense of serenity enfolded them as they entered a new part of their life. God had sent help when they needed it, often in the form of strangers who had the courage to reach out to others.

Debbie had opened the door that day in the parking lot with her offer to help; then Will, outgoing and strong and with so many stories to tell; Rita with her rosary, who had come to sit and pray; and the St. Paul's respite group members—Ruth, Mary Maud, and Janice—who were so kind, dependable, and capable. The gift that each one brought had been just right; and when employed in Christian love, it had encompassed both the giver and the receiver in the warm circle of God's love.

EPILOGUE

June Ryan now serves on the board of the Tallahassee Alzheimer's Project, Inc., and speaks to groups about the disease. June plays the part of the Alzheimer's patient in skits to train volunteers. She appears on local television shows to discuss hints for the care of the patient, and has volunteered to receive phone calls from other caregivers of Alzheimer's patients who need someone to talk with. Elyse now works at St. Paul's respite project as a social worker and serves as the assistant director. ❖

Jackie

MOTHER. THE LITTLE GIRL MOUTHED THE WORD SILENTLY as she sat beside her sleeping mother's bed in a tiny efficiency apartment in Brooklyn, New York. The year was 1938. At the age of six, Jackie Page's restraint was remarkable. The last of her crayons, and her only entertainment for the next four hours, had slipped from her fingers and rolled just out of reach. Because Jackie's mother, Gladys, slept in the daytime and worked at night, she had trained Jackie to ask for what she wanted before she went to sleep. Jackie wasn't about to wake her up.

Gladys was a private-duty nurse who had been raised in an orphanage. She had anxiously awaited Jackie's birth—her child would be the first real family she had ever known. That anticipation and excitement quickly turned to confusion when, for the first twenty-four hours, the nurses brought Jackie to her wrapped in blankets up to her neck. Gladys had undergone emergency surgery when Jackie was born, and her doctors did not want to break the news that Jackie would be totally dependent the rest of her life. No one said anything, but Gladys suspected that something was terribly wrong.

No one at the small hospital in Asheville, North Carolina, could tell Gladys or her husband, John, what was wrong with Jackie. Gladys cried for three months, and then decided she had to get help. Doctors from a Shrine Hospital two hours away held a local orthopedic clinic once each month. Gladys took Jackie to the clinic where doctors told her, "There is nothing we can do. You need to go to New York to have access to specialists."

In New York City, Gladys and John learned that Jackie had arthrogryposis multiplex congenita, a congenital disease with an unknown cause. The doctors explained that Jackie would be a quadriplegic because all of her joints were fused into a fixed, bent position. Individuals with the disease tended to have limbs that were tubular, as well as underdeveloped muscles. She would never move any of her extremities, and her condition would require extensive surgery throughout her childhood. Surgeons performed several operations on Jackie's hands to release them from their tightly twisted grip—but each time the braces came off, they returned to their original position.

The Pages decided to make New York their home so Jackie could receive the care she needed. They provided toys and games to keep the neighborhood kids interested in coming to visit, but all too soon the children hit the bicycle age and increasingly left Jackie alone.

Four or five years later, surgery for a double spinal fusion robbed Jackie of the little bit of hand movement she had and put her in a body cast for a year. It was also the occasion of her grandmother's first visit and the beginning of inventions to make Jackie more self-sufficient. Persons had given Jackie several back scratchers while she was in the hospital, an ingenious way of scratching maddening itches. Grandma, seeing that Jackie was unable to perform the smallest task—even that of turning the page of a book—without assistance, suggested, "Why not use a back scratcher in your mouth to turn pages?"

"Gee, this works great," Jackie told her grandmother after a few days of practice.

JACKIE MET HER EDUCATIONAL REQUIREMENTS AT HOME. The school board assigned a teacher to instruct Jackie three days a week for one and one-half hours. Her mother drilled her on spelling, and Jackie figured out her own method of doing arithmetic. She spent only one morning with her grammar school class, and that was the morning of her graduation.

High school was more of the same home schooling, with a teacher coming to the apartment just two times a week for an hour and a half. Jackie's world was narrow. It consisted of school, books, trips to the park, and visits with her parents' friends. She was the first home student installed in the high school Arista Honor Society. On graduation day, three honor society representatives and three other students from the school arrived to help her celebrate her graduation. She'd never seen them before and never saw them again.

Only days after graduation, eighteen-year-old Jackie sat in her chair and stared out at a world that seemed to have no place for her. Graduation had launched her high-school counterparts headlong into their plans for life—searching for jobs, applying to colleges, serving in the armed forces, or getting married.

"What are your plans?" one of the honor society students had asked her brightly at her home graduation.

"Just, . . . just to be at home," she'd said, feeling stupid. Someone from vocational rehabilitation had come to the apartment to help her figure out what type of work she could do at home. "I'm sorry," the woman said, as Jackie steeled herself for disappointing news. "Because you have hand limitations, there's nothing you can do."

After graduation, Gladys didn't explore social and vocational opportunities for Jackie. Jackie was now four feet tall and weighed about fifty-eight pounds. Her rare condition had come at a time when no family support groups or role models were available. Jackie spent the next five years of her life in virtual seclusion—reading, listening to television and radio shows, and praying for an end to her isolation.

At this point, having a friend or a volunteer come a few hours each week to sit with Jackie regularly would have benefited the whole family. Her parents needed to pursue other activities together to strengthen their bond, and Jackie needed to build new relationships and to move toward independence.

JACKIE WATCHED FROM HER WHEELCHAIR as her mother unpacked a box of glassware and stacked the glasses in the cupboards. The grass is always greener somewhere else to an alcoholic; and Nashville, Tennessee, with a few relatives looked great to her dad. John had come home one night and proclaimed, "You can't sell anything in New York." He then announced his plans to move the family.

"Mom, I wonder if they have a Junior League here that supplies books for people with disabilities?" Jackie asked, as her mother took a break to feed her. She wondered if Nashville held anything more for her than the same deadening emptiness—an emptiness she tried to fill with books mailed free by the Junior League.

ELSA ELLIS SLOWLY REREAD JACKIE'S LETTER requesting an organization or program that could help her find friends and activities as
well as library services for persons with disabilities. The letter didn't
tell Elsa much—only that Jackie Page was new to Nashville. Different
agencies had forwarded the letter until it reached Elsa, a member of
Belmont Methodist Church.

"We've got someone to visit," Elsa told her husband, Henry. It
was January. Elsa, now five months pregnant, was committed in her
efforts to involve the church in ministry to individuals with disabling
conditions.

HENRY and ELSA had met at Belmont Methodist Church, where
they now planned to take Jackie. Henry, a resident auditor at Sewart
Air Force Base, had heard of Belmont's minister, Dr. John Rustin, and
had come to visit one Sunday. While at the church, he met Elsa, a
student at the University of Tennessee School of Social Work.

Elsa was carrying a load of books and pamphlets to distribute at
the evening meeting, which she was leading. Henry offered to carry
the books and asked about the program as they walked to the
fellowship hall. Elsa explained that little was being done by either the
government or the church to assure the human and civil rights of
disabled persons. She felt that the church was the place to start with
public involvement, so she was leading a series of programs on the
church's responsibility to include persons with disabilities in the full
fellowship of the church.

"It is important to prepare the way before dropping persons with
disabilities into a new situation," she told him. "This is an easy way to
get information across—it allows the audience to get more comfortable
with the various disabilities. A period of questions and answers allows
those individuals who are most comfortable to interact with the
speakers, some of whom are disabled themselves. They get to know
them as persons."

"That's an exciting concept," Henry had agreed.

ELSA AND HENRY DROVE TO THE ADDRESS listed on the envelope that
same day. Henry rapped on the door one last time, giving Elsa a
questioning look. "I know someone's home," Elsa whispered. "Let's
leave a note." Hurriedly she scribbled, *We're from Belmont Methodist
Church and think you would enjoy attending. Please call us.* She signed

their names, added a telephone number and address, and pushed it through the mail slot in the heavy oak door.

Jackie, unable to answer the door, watched from her seat near the window as the couple climbed into an old Rambler and drove away. Her father had gone downtown to the Methodist church for services. Her mother, who still worked nights at local hospitals, was sound asleep in the back bedroom.

"Someone left something," she called to her father as he unlocked the front door.

"It's a note," John said, opening it for Jackie to read.

Humph, little do they know, thought the lonely young woman as she read their invitation. She'd lost hope of escaping her dreary lifestyle. *This is a nice little dream, but I'll write them a note about my physical problems.* At age twenty-four, stomach troubles and sleeping difficulties plagued her. Her problems stemmed from her greatest foes—boredom and loneliness.

Always practical, Jackie painstakingly scribbled out a reply with a pencil clamped between her teeth. The note ended with the words, *Mother works most Sundays, and the only way for me to ride in a car is to sit between the passenger and the door. Thank you for your interest, but as you can see, going to church is impossible.*

Three nights later, as Jackie ate supper, the telephone rang.

"It's Elsa," her mother said, putting her hand over the mouthpiece. "She and Henry want to come and visit. She says they can work something out to get you to church." Jackie had heard many token offers over the years.

"Ask her to come," Jackie said, willing to hear them out.

THE NEXT NIGHT, ELSA AND HENRY STOPPED BY THE PAGE HOME. Through the sheer living room curtain, they saw a young woman seated in a wheelchair watching a small black and white television.

"There's no reason for her to be alone and just sitting," Henry whispered to Elsa. Elsa nodded, warmed by Henry's response.

The Ellises sipped coffee and looked from Mr. Page, who was busy trying to impress them with his sales abilities, to Jackie, a tiny woman with a deep, resonant voice. Elsa with her deep red hair and Henry whose black hair was just beginning to thin were both in their early forties. Both were on the short side, and to Jackie they seemed unlikely Good Samaritans. Her hesitation at their enthusiastic invitation neither surprised nor dismayed Elsa or Henry.

The church to which Henry and Elsa invited Jackie was working to become a caring congregation. The Ellises realized the church was not fully accessible for Jackie's wheelchair. But a caring nucleus of church members had undergone training and would welcome Jackie and her family. The training had helped the members examine their own attitudes of rejection, fear, and avoidance. It had covered many of the basics: to sit down if possible to talk to persons in wheelchairs, to avoid leaning on the chair, to ask before pushing the wheelchair, to speak directly to the individual, and to make sure someone is always with the visitor.

The positive response of Belmont members to Elsa's programs made the Ellises confident that the members would welcome Jackie and include her in the full fellowship of the church. All that remained was for Jackie to agree.

ELSA DECIDED THE BEST WAY TO START was to tell Jackie about herself. "I was raised by parents who valued people for who they were. Their differences didn't matter. My grandparents lived with us, and Grandpa couldn't tie his shoes. It was my responsibility from childhood on to tie my grandfather's shoes. My great-aunt was deaf and didn't read sign language. We had to yell at her to communicate. "If you really want to do something, you can find a way," my parents assured me. My Great-aunt Mamie 'listened' to our violin and piano by touching her teeth to the instruments. It never occurred to me that her unusual method was anything but normal."

Jackie returned Elsa's warm smile, aware that she was receiving two of God's most precious gifts through this woman: acceptance and belonging. Here was someone she could admire, someone who seemed to mean business.

"We have just completed a series of programs at Belmont on the church's responsibility to include persons with disabling conditions in the full fellowship of the church," Elsa continued. "Now we're incorporating those concepts into an ongoing community-wide program we call Outlook Nashville. We think you'll enjoy it, and we need your help." Henry pulled a brochure from his jacket and opened it so Jackie could read it: "Outlook Nashville, Inc., Opportunities for the [Disabled]. A non-profit, educational, charitable organization.

Created to promote better understanding and acceptance of persons who are mentally, physically, or emotionally disabled. To explore unmet needs, and to motivate the community to meet these needs."

Elsa saw Jackie's eyes blur with tears that she hastily blinked back. She wondered how much suppressed anger for the years of neglect and isolation lay beneath Jackie's calm exterior.

"This looks interesting," Jackie said. The brochure pictured children with disabilities participating in weekly creative expression exercises under the guidance of a local radio and television personality, kids camping with Lookouts and their families, a pilot telephone/TV program for children with various disabilities, and Lookouts viewing the same program in their homes.

"What are Lookouts?" Mr. Page asked, his face softening into an interested smile.

"A Lookout is a nonprofessional person, either disabled or non-disabled, who demonstrates an interest in our outreach program by taking the basic training course. He or she then 'looks out' for the needs of families with disabled members in the community," Elsa said.

"What do you think, Jackie?" Henry asked. "Would you like to come to church with us?"

It was 1955, a time when being different didn't fit into the American ideal. Jackie's heart was pounding as all eyes turned toward her. Here was a chance to meet some new people. Yet, her feelings were ambivalent. Although her parents had met her physical needs, she had been born at a time when a positive self-concept for individuals with disabling conditions was made more difficult by the negative responses of the world at large.

Two persons sat before Jackie, asking her to believe that something good would come of the risk.

"Yes," she responded. "I'll give it a try."

ELSA SMILED BROADLY AS JOHN wheeled Jackie into Belmont Methodist Church for the first time. The quiet woman they'd met four days earlier was gone. Here was a smiling young woman, dressed in a tan wool suit with a white blouse accented with a pearl circle pin on the lapel. In a matter of days, Jackie's identity had already begun to emerge.

"You look wonderful." Elsa complimented her new friend, nodding at Mr. Page, who explained he was going to pick up Gladys during the Sunday school hour and would return for worship.

"He seemed a little hesitant to leave you," Elsa said as Henry pushed Jackie toward an appropriate age-level Sunday school class.

"It's my first activity away from home without my parents," Jackie informed them.

As they moved slowly through the crowded hallway, several persons came over to meet the visitor.

"Are you from Nashville?" asked one. When he learned that she had recently moved from New York, he told of his visit to the Empire State building.

"I hope you'll come to our Wednesday night supper," another new acquaintance invited. "Elsa is putting on some terrific programs."

By the time they arrived at Jackie's classroom, the threesome had broken the ice. Jackie was delighted with her new friends, and Henry and Elsa admired Jackie's spunk. Mutual risk and trust were at work to plant the seeds of friendship.

In the college age Sunday school classroom, Elsa introduced Jackie to those present. "Hi, I'm Jean," said one young woman. "It's a little chilly near the windows. Would you like to sit with me over here?"

When Elsa saw that Jackie was enjoying hearing about Jean's work as an artist, she announced, "I'm going to my class now. I'll be back to pick you up later."

An hour later as Elsa and Henry made their way back toward the college age class, they caught sight of Jackie's parents arriving for church services.

"Where's Jackie?" John demanded, concerned that this couple had abandoned their defenseless daughter. Just then the college and career classroom door burst open and out came Jackie, pushed by Jean and surrounded by laughing young men and women. Elsa felt herself lifted by the moment and winked at Henry. "You open a door for Jackie, and she goes through it."

Jackie was growing, pushing at the limits long imposed by overprotective parents and a community that seemed to have no place for her. This was a new community, and already she was proving that she had much to share with other people.

"ELSA. . . . " THE TONE IN JACKIE'S VOICE made Elsa stop her supper preparation and sit down with Jackie, who was visiting for the afternoon.

"Elsa, class members teach my Sunday school class, and they want to know if I'll prepare a lesson."

Elsa felt her unborn child give a huge kick. She was anticipating the baby's arrival in another month. In a sense, Jackie was being born also—despite her serious physical limitations. Opportunities were opening up for Jackie. Members of the Sunday school class had begun to take Jackie places—dinners out, to the bowling alley and the theater. Jackie was an intelligent, articulate young woman looking for a place in the world. During the past three months, she'd moved beyond the disabilities to the ability.

"What's the problem?"

"I've never taught a Sunday school class."

"Is there anything you think they need to know?"

"Well, yes."

"Then teach them!" Elsa found that many persons with disabilities had much to say but were never given an opportunity. Later Elsa enlisted Jackie's aid in a Sunday night program at Belmont to promote the need to reestablish Goodwill Industries in Nashville.

"I'm scared," Jackie whispered to Elsa. She'd worked for a week on her five-minute talk, but this territory was new. The tight knot in her stomach reminded her that she had agreed to something she wasn't sure she could deliver.

"What if I fall flat on my face?"

Elsa looked into Jackie's frightened eyes and smiled reassuringly. "There will always be someone there to pick you up. You don't have to worry. We all fall on our faces. So what?"

A hush fell over the room as Elsa wheeled Jackie to the microphone. Elsa returned to her seat. Jackie took a deep breath and then leaned forward to read from her notes, which Elsa had laid on the lectern. She tried not to show her dismay when she realized that the microphone was hiding part of her notes. Instead, she looked around the microphone and did the best she could, rushing through the speech in just under three minutes.

"It was horrible," she moaned to Elsa the next day.

"Actually, you were pretty darn good," Elsa said. "I was proud of you."

A part-time state director of the Easter Seal Society had been in the audience. A few days later, Jackie received an encouraging letter from him: "You seem to have found your niche in life, talking in public." Jackie was incredulous—the man had recognized a gift that she would have discounted entirely. In the following year, Jackie would speak to more than 1,000 people in a successful effort to return Goodwill Industries to Nashville.

Speaking became one of Jackie's strengths. The Wednesday night church program committee invited her to speak on disabilities as part of a panel discussion. "She's always willing to take a dare," Elsa whispered to Henry, full of pride at Jackie's accomplishments.

JACKIE WAS BLOOMING, BECOMING A WHOLE PERSON. With that personhood came a hunger for information beyond the simple recreational reading materials she'd used to fill her idle hours. Jackie's appetite for Elsa's old college sociology and psychology textbooks and her fascination with new concepts thrilled Elsa.

"Let's talk about the role that public opinion plays in the political process," Jackie would say as she settled into the Ellises' car. Or a phone call from Elsa while her newborn son, Jamie, napped would begin, "I think whether or not an individual conforms in a group stems from . . . " and Jackie would take off, bouncing ideas past Elsa without so much as a how do you do.

Elsa smiled and listened as Jackie reveled in her new found world of ideas. For some time, she and Henry had talked about Jackie's need for further education. They had discussed this idea informally with counselors from vocational rehabilitation but could not convince them that Jackie was college material. They would have to be *shown*.

That night Elsa and Jackie talked in the Page living room, now cluttered with psychology books. "Jackie, what would you think about taking a psychology course one night a week with Henry?"

"That's a nice dream, but they took one look at me in New York and said, forget it," Jackie said, shaking her head.

Jackie's negativity was normal. One way to survive after having your hopes dashed repeatedly is to become skeptical.

But Elsa wasn't about to toss out the idea. Several evenings later, as Henry sipped sweetened tea in the Page kitchen, he struck a deal with Jackie and her grandmother who had come to live with them.

Henry had a bachelor's degree but enjoyed taking night classes at the University of Tennessee Extension School to increase his accounting skills. He thought taking a psychology class might be fun. He could take Jackie and find out how she would rank with other students. "If your grandmother will make me biscuits and cornbread, I'll be happy to take you to class."

Jackie was overwhelmed but determined to do her best. "Now that you're going to be a college student, you'll be needing this," Henry said, placing an old, beat-up IBM typewriter before her. He laughed as her eyes grew wide in amazement. "It seems to me that you could use your dowel mouth stick and learn to type."

Jackie looked from Henry to the typewriter. She located the "on" switch and flipped it with her dowel stick. Then she typed out the message: THANK YOU, HENRY. I THINK I CAN!

Jackie was accepted to the night school class and began to learn the typewriter keys. When the Introduction to Psychology class began, Henry took notes, and Jackie typed them. Jackie learned how to outline by following Henry's example. As she added facts and figures that Henry had omitted, Jackie discovered that she had an excellent memory. Gradually students began to strike up conversations with her, groaning over tests or looking forward to their next semester of classes.

It was the most exciting summer of Jackie's life. Attending college had been a secret dream. She had always wanted to go to college; but she knew her family couldn't afford to send her, so she never mentioned her desires.

The Ellises' belief in Jackie's abilities and enthusiasm for her intellect gave Jackie the courage to try new things—to risk both success and failure. She'd even overcome her shyness enough to ask Elsa if she could spend a few days at their home while her parents took a vacation.

"Of course," Elsa said, knowing the amount of care Jackie needed. "Besides, I want to talk with you about something."

Two weeks later, Jackie spent her first night in the care of someone other than her mother. Countless conversations with Elsa had finally reassured her mother that someone else could meet Jackie's needs.

Elsa learned how to work with Jackie. She fed Jackie her meals when they were out, got her into and out of her wheelchair, and benefited from Jackie's ability to graciously lead a caregiver through the steps necessary to accomplish a given task. Jackie had spent a lifetime in her own skin and knew a good deal about getting her needs met. Elsa was a warm, friendly, and willing aide.

Elsa's home was cozy and inviting. Little Jamie's playpen stood in the living room. Just watching him bat at his mobiles or break into a smile when he made eye contact was sweet entertainment for Jackie. After Elsa fed the baby, she bathed him, and then tucked him into his crib. "I hope you like fried chicken," Henry said as Jackie watched. "I think I'm doing this right."

"First dip it in the milk, then roll it in flour with salt and pepper," Jackie advised. "And make sure the grease is good and hot before you lay the chicken in the skillet."

"You're the boss," Henry said with a grin.

IT WAS LATE WHEN ELSA FINISHED HELPING JACKIE PREPARE for bed. The disease that caused the joints in all of Jackie's limbs to be fixed called for creativity when it came to fashioning a comfortable bed.

"You're like the princess and the pea," Elsa said, as Jackie directed the placement of a half dozen pillows around her so she could sleep. Jackie seized the moment to ask Elsa a question that had been on her mind for a long time. "Can I come to live with you when my parents die?"

Elsa stopped arranging pillows, composing herself for the answer she must give. Many of the kids at Outlook Nashville had asked her that same question. She had not always been able to assure them that they could create their own future. The young woman before her was different.

"Jackie, Henry and I are willing to help you prepare yourself for a future. I know you're smart. I rely on you so much. You've been a great sounding board as we've developed programs at Outlook. When I've felt like I was sinking, you just looked for another angle. Now we need to look for another angle for you. If you don't get an education, you'll be dependent your whole life. You've shown that you can do college work. I want to take you down tomorrow for an interview with the dean of admissions at Peabody and see about getting you accepted as a full-time college student."

Jackie's head was spinning with the enormity of Elsa's gift. Looking back, she realized that the interview was the beginning of her march toward self-determination. Rather than supporting Jackie's dependency by promising to be her caregiver, Elsa encouraged Jackie to move toward independence and self-reliance.

That night Jackie let herself dream of a future in which she was in command. Elsa had challenged her and given her a new vision, knowing full well that vision and hope keep us alive.

Elsa was able to support Jackie in ways her mother could not. Elsa understood the discouragement that came from being turned down by one agency after another. She offered to help Jackie through the maze of the Nashville service system. This navigation is an appropriate role for caregivers.

THE NEXT MORNING, THE TWO WOMEN SAT IN THE DEAN'S outer office as a mahogany clock chimed the hour. Young men in khaki pants and women in billowing skirts and sweaters ambled across the campus. Jackie, dressed in an attractive navy blue suit, her dark hair cut fashionably short, clenched her teeth and waited.

"Why do you want to go to college?" the admissions officer asked, opening Jackie's file.

Jackie smiled brightly. She and Elsa had rehearsed her response. "The only thing you can train about me is my mind. You can't train my hands. You can't train my feet. I need an education to become self-sufficient."

He looked at her transcript, then pulled out a clean sheet of paper and made a few notes. "We'll accept you as a special student," he said, standing up. "Bring me your schedule each quarter, and we'll see about moving your classes to the first floor."

Both Jackie and Elsa laughed like school girls as Elsa lifted Jackie from her wheelchair into her car, and strapped her in.

"How am I going to pay for this?" Jackie asked.

"We'll go to the Division of Rehabilitation Services first. It's an arm of the federal government that provides evaluation and training for persons with disabilities. If that doesn't work, I'll go to the Easter Seal Society."

Rehabilitation Services did turn Jackie down when she had been unable to tell them what job she would perform upon graduation. "Nonfeasible for college," Rehab told her as she and Elsa argued her case at the local office.

As Elsa pushed Jackie down the institutional green hallway, the young woman insisted, "There has to be a way."

"I believe there is," Elsa replied.

At a board meeting of the Easter Seal Society that same week, Elsa outlined Jackie's situation. The board awarded Jackie tuition for her freshman year at Peabody College. Elsa came home from the meeting flushed with excitement. "Jackie Page, you are going to college!" she announced ceremoniously.

ANOTHER HOT SOUTHERN SUMMER WAS ENDING as Jackie and her parents rode home. Her parents' week-long vacation had improved the mood of the whole family. Her dad was even whistling.

"I've been accepted at Peabody College and the tuition is already paid, so it won't cost you a thing," she blurted out at last.

Jackie's parents stiffened. After a long silence, her mother replied, "Well, if you think you can do it . . . ," letting her voice trail off. Mr. Page said nothing.

As the taillights of the Page family car disappeared down the street, Henry slipped his arm around his wife's waist. "Congratulations," he said with a grin.

"She deserves what every other adult deserves—an opportunity to make choices and to act on them."

A paper on self-determination from the National Information Center for Children and Youth with Handicaps (NICHCY) emphasizes that people with disabilities need to "live with dignity and respect; to have the same opportunities to fail and to succeed as people without disabilities; and to no longer be seen as individuals perpetually dependent on welfare and charity."

Jackie did not want to attend college just to say she'd been to school. The college experience was to equip her for work with people with various disabling conditions. For that purpose, she chose sociology as a major to furnish the necessary working concepts and an English minor to provide the tools of expression.

"She'll need someone to get her around campus," Henry added. "I don't think you can count on anyone's doing it out of the goodness of his or her heart on a regular basis."

"You're right," Elsa agreed. "I plan to bring it up at church. Maybe a class will participate at some level to pay for an aide. We need to help Jackie get her education, so she won't wind up institutionalized when something happens to her parents."

The next Sunday Elsa presented Jackie's dreams to an older singles class at the church. Several of the members knew Jackie. Glad for the opportunity to help, the class voted to provide funds for the small fee charged by another Belmont Church member to push Jackie around campus and feed her lunch.

THE FIRST YEAR PRESENTED ENORMOUS CHALLENGES TO JACKIE. She'd never been in a library, had never seen a bibliography, and her reading speed was pitiful. Once classes started, she realized that the things she'd learned to get her general diploma wouldn't help with her college classes. Still, she had a chance, and she wasn't going to give up. Instead she gave up all outside activities except worship and settled in for a grueling year.

"How's it going?" Elsa asked one week into Jackie's first semester. Elsa had stopped off at a local bakery to pick up "junk food" to celebrate this new milestone. She wanted Jackie to know that even while so many firsts were happening, she was available just to listen and encourage.

Elsa enjoyed Jackie's company and her wry sense of humor. It was fun to see her having successes. Life with Jackie was exciting for everyone. She was challenging long-held theories about what severely disabled persons could do—and she was winning.

"How's it going?" Jackie replied, surveying the stack of books on the dining room table. "If you want to find me, look for a green glow, because I'm the greenest first-year student they've ever had."

Though Jackie struggled, the measures taken by faculty members on her behalf encouraged Jackie. The dean of admissions had made good on his offer to request that professors move their classes to the first floor of their buildings. A few professors protested the move. One refused because of his classroom setup. He offered instead to pull Jackie's wheelchair up the flight of steps.

Several students in Jackie's neighborhood, including a retired Navy man, took her to school and brought her home. She took paper and carbon paper to class and asked a good student to share his or her notes. Jackie knew who to ask to write the essay portion of her tests. College provided both academic training and life training as Jackie learned the mechanics of getting her needs met.

The next year Jackie again approached the local rehabilitation office for tuition money. "You are nonfeasible, and the case is closed," she was told. "Even if you do get a degree, who would hire you?" By watching Elsa at work, Jackie had learned to be her own advocate. She knew the state rehabilitation offices also were located in Nashville. "I want this decision reviewed at the state office," she replied. "Who do I call?"

Jackie set up an appointment to discuss college feasibility. When she arrived, her records were laid on the desk before her, stamped NONFEASIBLE. "I'll bet those records don't tell you that I type and use the telephone, or that I am a public speaker. It really bothers me that rehabilitation doesn't believe in its own philosophy that each individual should have the opportunity to develop his or her capacities to the fullest. I've already proved I can do college work by finishing my first year at Peabody.

"Who's going to take care of me? I have no brothers and sisters. My parents won't live forever. Without an education, I could be at the state mental institution or in a developmental disabilities institution or a county nursing home using taxes instead of paying taxes when they are gone." Jackie left the office with full tuition and money for textbooks.

Elsa was learning too. When Jackie complained, "Aw, that was a terrible test," Elsa's first reaction was, "Oh, you shouldn't say that. Don't tell other people you feel that way." She worried that others would think Jackie couldn't succeed. "I've got to be honest," Jackie replied. "I get upset like anybody else. So why should I be different ?"

GRADUATION DAY DAWNED COOL AND SUNNY; a gentle breeze fluttered through the dogwoods. Gladys Page pulled a comb through her hair, closed the clasp on a string of imitation pearls, and went to check on Jackie. At age thirty, her daughter had accomplished more than she had ever dreamed possible, thanks to the love and care of Elsa, Henry, and the other members of Belmont Methodist Church. "You've done so much, Jackie," she told her daughter as she applied Jackie's makeup. "You know, I was afraid for you to go to college. It hurt me to think of people staring at you or being mean to you."

Jackie thought a minute. "Mother, you're right. They did stare at first. Why wouldn't they stare? But they were never mean. We'd better get going."

Jackie Page, dressed in the black cap and gown of every other Peabody College graduate, watched from her vantage point to the right of the dais. Each graduate ascended the twenty steps to the platform where the college president and other dignitaries stood, conferring degrees. "Jacquelyn Forrest Page," intoned the president, and Jackie experienced the elation that comes from setting a goal and attaining it. In four short years, she had lost the green glow and had earned a degree in sociology.

JACKIE WAS ACCEPTED INTO THE MASTER'S PROGRAM at Peabody in guidance and counseling. Though Rehab had served notice that it would not fund any more of Jackie's education, her church presented her with a money tree. That money, along with money from the government for individuals with disabilities, funded her master's degree.

Elsa scolded Jackie for her lack of emotion when presented with the money tree, "Jackie, we're going to have to work on your showing emotion."

"If I get too emotional I'll cry, and that means someone else will have to wipe my eyes and my nose. Besides, if I get too excited, they may think they are doing too much—and quit!"

The outdoor graduation for Jackie's master's degree was rained out and hastily moved to Belmont Methodist Church. Jackie received the wrong cap and gown, but it didn't matter—she had reached her goal.

While in graduate school, Jackie had helped write a grant for Outlook Nashville, including the job description for coordinator of training. The grant came through in the late spring while she was finishing her master's degree, and Jackie became the coordinator of training.

The diagnosis of lung cancer for John Page and his death soon after brought more changes to Jackie and her mother. Gladys had devoted her life to her husband and daughter and now was struggling with her loss. Jackie and Elsa tried to figure out how to help. They decided to enlist Gladys's skills for Outlook. "Gladys, would you consider acting as a family consultant in ceramics and help the participants assume some responsibility for using the sale of the finished products to help support the program? They need to learn to give as well as receive," Elsa said.

"I've never done ceramics," Gladys admitted. In fact, Gladys had few outside activities. She didn't enjoy cards or gossip.

"A ceramics group is going to meet in a little bit. Would you try it and consider working with the group?" Elsa invited.

By the end of the morning, Gladys had finished a tiny Christmas boot and had discovered that she loved ceramics. She agreed to become the ceramics consultant for the Lookouts.

In 1967 Jackie and Elsa coauthored the *Lookout Training Course: Manual for Instructors*. Lloyd Dunn, Ph.D. and chair of the Department of Special Education at George Peabody College for Teachers, wrote the following in the FOREWORD:

> Perhaps the greatest need today is to develop and test innovative ways of opening the doors still further for individuals and groups with the rare ability to conceive of new approaches, and with the drive and commitment to put them to the test of implementation.
>
> One of the best examples of this is Outlook Nashville. In the twelve years since its inception, it has established an array of creative ways of demonstrating how a community can better serve persons who are [disabled]. . . .
>
> Nashville and the Nation owe a great debt to the flame of leadership which is represented by Elsa T. Ellis, M.S.S.W., Executive Director of Outlook Nashville. Mrs. Ellis is a rare individual; she has ideas; she has drive; she has organizational talent; and she has the persistence to follow through. . . .
>
> Teaming up with her has been Jacquelyn Page, M.A., as Coordinator of Training. In spite of severe physical handicaps, including quadriplegia, she has demonstrated that physical prowess is not a necessary prerequisite to important human endeavor. Under her tutelage, the LOOKOUT Training Course—repeated and refined many times in the past seven years—has become an important force for changing attitudes, and helping non-professional persons to work better with the [disabled].

Jackie's work with Outlook Nashville brought meaning to her life. Her experiences—combined with her education—brought a special fervor, tempered with compassion and sensitivity to the organization. She writes in the manual: "All Trainees are *Human*. All need to be reassured throughout the course that the 10-hour course is just a beginning, to help them feel a little more comfortable. It is not expected to make them 'little therapists.' It is reassuring to trainees to learn that even professional workers are sometimes a little anxious before the first visit to a client."

The activities a Lookout could expect to participate in were varied. They are the same things any individual might wish to do: be friendlier; be an understanding neighbor; play with a disabled child; be a paid sitter or companion; tutor or assist homebound children with homework; discuss educational television programs by phone; participate in swimming, creative speech and drama, music, dance, crafts, or office experiences; teach crafts or special skills.

Perhaps most important to Jackie, who knew what it was like to be desperately lonely, was the opportunity to develop and coordinate training that culminated in Hi/Lo Camping for a group of people with disabilities and their families. Jackie and Gladys, along with other Outlook campers, planned to camp "Hi" in a motel room while "Lo" campers would live outdoors in tents or sleep out by the fire.

JACKIE WATCHED THE CHARACTERISTIC SMOKELIKE HAZE settle over the Great Smoky Mountains as children gathered fallen branches for the fire. The sounds of water rushing over mossy rocks and a woodland filled with red flowering rhododendrons against the backdrop of fragrant spruce and fir trees, made the trip a vacation for the senses. "It's good to be together," Elsa said, gathering up plates and cups.

The teenagers taught dance steps to one another—urging the adults to join in. One group was making plans to go bowling. Jackie passed the word that her group was heading to Cades Cove. Eddie announced that he had spotted blackberries and planned to pick enough for cobbler the next day. Lookout lifeguards taught swimming, and board members stimulated interest in fishing, archery, and dancing.

All around her, Jackie saw the group members come alive as they experienced warmth, acceptance, and activity. They had planned the mid-June camp to avoid the summer rush and had filled the days with shared unstructured activities. Publicity had gone out to Lookouts and to families with members with disabling conditions. Churches, civic groups, and radio spots promoted the event. Informal activities included watermelon cutting, wiener and marshmallow roasts, sing-alongs, and conversation around the huge campfire that burned all night.

When Jackie awoke the next morning atop her pile of pillows, she could hear high-pitched, excited voices outside. She smiled contentedly. Although camping really wasn't her thing, the joy the others were experiencing made her happy too.

Only as Jackie typed the Outlook newsletter, composed of stories written on scraps of paper by all the campers, did she learn how much camping had meant to the group: eight pages of observations testified to the foundations laid for friendships. Evalene reflected on her camping experience—an experience made possible because people cared.

> Oh, this must be a fantastic dream, but it can be done if enough people, like the Clarks at Tuckaleechee Village really care and are interested. I have the feeling that a lot of people really do care but they, like me three years ago, just never thought of it. The Clarks are doing wonderful things to make it possible for [disabled] persons to enjoy vacations in the Smokies with our families. The smiling faces around here reflect their happiness. . . . It is impossible to put our feelings into words. . . . We feel like somebody again . . . loved, wanted, and doing things we felt were gone from us forever in this lifetime. . . . We are living again because someone cared and gave us hope.

The decade of the seventies was a time of change for both the Page and Ellis families. Gladys Page inherited a piece of property in Asheville, North Carolina, which she could receive only if she lived on the property one year. Henry and Elsa agreed that it was time to move nearer to Elsa's aging parents in Orlando, Florida.

After moving to North Carolina, it took Jackie nearly a year to find a job. She became the director of a twenty-county Easter Seal Society. She represented disabled persons and their families throughout western North Carolina.

In the late seventies, Jackie and Gladys returned to Nashville to be closer to friends, family, and better employment opportunities. Unable to find employment, Jackie became a volunteer advocate for individuals with disabilities, and three years later was hired as the director of the mayor's office for disabled persons in metropolitan

Nashville. In an article for *Response* magazine entitled "Moving Out of Society's Back Rooms," Jackie writes,

> Churches should assume the role of prime mover for advocacy. My personal life was turned around because a church and its members reached out to me offering me love and acceptance as well as a chance to gain skills I needed to become an advocate for myself and others.
>
> Numerous national church leaders agreed with this viewpoint in their meeting at an ad hoc committee at the White House Conference. They recommended, among other things, that churches actively recruit disabled persons into the ministry, eliminate physical barriers that prevent disabled individuals from participating in church programs, provide consciousness-raising experiences for church congregations to ease the entrance of (disabled) persons into overall church life and become stronger advocates in the fight for full civil rights of disabled individuals.

Unless a disabled person is present, the church often shows little initiative in regard to special needs persons. Jackie was named to a United Methodist task force under a section of the Board of Global Ministries whose work moved the church toward becoming more inclusive. The task force's work culminated in public hearings around the country. The United Methodist Church eventually incorporated recommendations of the task force into the *Book of Discipline*.

A CHRISTMAS LETTER FROM JACKIE IN 1980 brought discouraging news to Elsa and Henry. Jackie began, "Nineteen eighty has been a rough year for both Mom and I, six live-ins, upsets at the office." Jackie's mother was now 72. They had had six live-in aides. One was a pathological liar and had used Jackie's VISA card without authorization. A rash of other difficulties were enough to blight the excitement of Jackie's purchase of her own condominium in 1979.

January 9, 1981, Gladys Page died suddenly from a virus that had weakened her heart. Jackie found herself alone just as she had told rehabilitation services and colleges she would be one day. With her dearest friends twelve hours away by car and her job keeping her anchored in Nashville, Jackie had several choices: to live in a nursing home or to hire a full-time companion and request help when needed.

Jackie realized that now she must pay to receive care at all times. No one would be caring for her out of the goodness of his or her heart. She chose to employ an aide.

In 1982 Jackie attended a public hearing of the state school board as a spectator to hear discussions on special education. The next morning she was on the front page of the Nashville *Tennessean*, unable to keep silent as members argued over the use of funds to educate severely disabled students. "Don't be so absorbed in trying to come up with rules and regulations that we prevent individuals from receiving an education that is their full right, because of the way they look and act. Don't assume, as people did when I was born, that I was so limited, why not let me die. This is still going on, even in this enlightened time."

Jackie was in the public eye—even making the headlines—but her personal life was often in turmoil. When her companion left to undertake new challenges, Jackie had to find a new companion immediately. Arrangements lasted only three months. Fortunately a relief person and friend became available. In later years, Jackie relied on others who did not have her best interests at heart. Funds transferred from her accounts left her woefully short and scrambling to make up for overdrafts created by a dishonest aide.

Jackie's work continued to play an important role in her life. Working with the Mayor's Advisory Committee for Handicapped Persons, Jackie, volunteers, and fellow staffers compiled a 650-entry "Access to Nashville" guide. They also conducted the second annual Awareness Week and worked with other groups to develop a better-coordinated system of services for persons with disabling conditions, including personal care attendants for those with severe physical disabilities.

Jackie's activities included work with Home 2, Inc., an agency that provided employment, housing, and transportation services to developmentally disabled folks. She also worked with the Nashville Urban League to improve opportunities for minorities and enhance transportation services for disabled and elderly. She continued her commitment to develop a disability awareness in her own church and to work with the Spinal Cord Injury Association locally. Truly, Jackie had become a powerful advocate for many people.

GERALDINE TERRY LAUGHED AND SHOOK HER HEAD as her longtime friend barked orders to direct her through the black night—up that street, take that road, get off the interstate here, loop around here, okay, we've made it. "Jackie, you are the best backseat driver I know," she said, pulling up to the valet parking stop at the Opryland Hotel.

Geraldine, a former university professor from Memphis, Tennessee, had come to Nashville several years earlier. She had accepted a position with the department of employment security when she couldn't find a teaching position. Her friendship with Jackie began as a professional acquaintance. Both were serving the community and had discovered through conversation that they both had an interest in sociology.

The election of Tennessee's new governor, LaMar Alexander, had created an opportunity for the two women to share a momentous occasion by attending an inaugural ball. A mutual friend had made two tickets available. "A lot of people don't dance so we won't be out of place," they agreed. Besides they'd never attended an inaugural ball before, and this was a unique opportunity.

Jackie's work required her to interact with public officials and stay abreast of what was happening in the political arena. As they entered the ballroom, Jackie saw several acquaintances. A band was playing, but most folks were visiting and making their way through a buffet line.

"I'm glad we came," said Geraldine.

"So am I," Jackie agreed. "If you'll get us a plate of food, I'll hold this table."

"Done," responded Geraldine.

AS A TEACHER, GERALDINE HAD WORKED WITH A FEW STUDENTS who were disabled. Though some were gracious, others were sour and hard to help, making the experience emotionally stressful. Jackie allowed Geraldine to feel comfortable in offering help.

"How do you know what to do?" a friend asked Geraldine one afternoon.

"It's just like dancing," Geraldine explained. "Some people are so clumsy, they step on your feet. Some lead you, and you never feel clumsy. Jackie takes your inexperience in stride and leads you."

The expense of a full-time aide kept Jackie's entertainment dollars at a minimum. Geraldine and Jackie discovered they could split an entree at lunch and be full. They planned lost-cost evenings at a local bookstore known for it's huge selection and small restaurant with frequent musical entertainment and author signings.

For Geraldine, going solo was no fun. Jackie's friendship, keen sense of humor, warmth, and compassion have enriched Geraldine's life. Since Jackie has no living relatives nearby, Geraldine always extends an invitation to join her own family at Christmas, along with an invitation to a foreign student. The last student, from Belgium, was amazed and enlightened when Geraldine brought out the cards and Jackie's card rack after the holiday meal. Now he will go home and share a new perspective on disability.

Along with Christmas, Geraldine works out surprise parties for her friend, making sure the restaurants have easy access for persons with disabilities. Jackie also enjoys entertaining. Her favorite show is "Great Chefs." With Geraldine acting as her hands, Jackie directs the preparation of the meal, recipe by recipe.

"ARE YOU SURE YOU WILL BE ALL RIGHT?" the driver of the Community Services van asked as he lowered the ramp. Jackie drove her power chair onto the sidewalk. She smiled and reassured him, "I'll be fine. I'll be ready to be picked up at 10 P.M. sharp." Then in typical Jackie fashion, she pressed the go switch that had been installed beside her left hand. She had just enough mobility to press the switch, which gave her access to a world of new places on her own. The continuous push for access by persons with disabilities had paid huge dividends for Jackie and millions of others whose physical limitations had previously caused them needless isolation.

As Jackie maneuvered her power chair through the crowd, stopping to chat with acquaintances, Jan and Dan walked in. "Hi, Jackie," they called when they spotted her.

Jackie breathed a sigh of relief. She worked hard to be independent; and after all these years, it was still difficult to ask for help. "Hi, Jan and Dan. Are you sitting anywhere special?"

"No. Would you care to join us?" Jan replied.

"I'd love to. Would you mind feeding me my meal?"

"Sure Jackie," Jan said as they followed Dan to a table.

"By the way, are you still receiving our church newsletter?" Dan asked, as salads and iced tea were set before them. Jackie did not attend the church that Dan was pastoring, but she had expressed an interest and began receiving the church newsletter.

"Yes. I keep reading about the choir. I've always wanted to sing in a church choir," she confided.

Jan beamed. "Oh, you can do that. Our choir is on the first floor. I'll be your choir buddy if you'd like and hold the music."

Church always had played a central part in Jackie's life, and she followed up on the invitation. Brookemeade Congregational Church had received recognition for its accessibility. Jan, who was not a choir member, followed through on her offer to sit next to Jackie and act as a choir buddy. "If I do this wrong, let me know," Jan said their first day at church. Jan's asking, "What's the best way?" allowed Jackie to express her needs openly.

JACKIE'S WILLINGNESS BOTH TO GIVE AND TO RECEIVE HELP has enriched her and her community. Recently, she'd agreed to be "roasted" by longtime friends to benefit Technology Access Center. She had served as the first president of its board. As Jackie prepared to leave the office, her telephone rang. She'd challenged a telephone technician to provide a switch that she could flip easily with her dowel stick. With the switch, she could answer the phone herself, positioning herself beside the receiver, which was attached to a telephone arm. By so doing, she could maintain the privacy of individuals, church representatives, government officials, and service organizations from Nashville, Washington, and places in between that called the Disability Information Office for Metropolitan Nashville.

"Jackie, can you take one more call before you go?" asked Fran, her associate. Jackie caught the tone in her voice. It signaled that someone who was struggling with a disability issue was on the other phone. Jackie had hundreds of these calls each month.

"Of course," she said, flipping her phone on. "This is Jackie Page. How may I help you?" The caller, who only heard Jackie's calm, resonant voice, could not know that the person speaking was someone who understood some of their terror; someone who knew the frustration, fear, and uncertainty that a disability brought. In Jackie, the callers reached someone resourceful. And because Jackie had lived a full, worthwhile life, she could reassure them that the possibility of bright days lay ahead for them too. She would not give up until she had helped them locate the necessary resources.

Jackie had told a woman just that morning, "Even though communication with agencies is better, and folks with disabilities are far more attuned and aggressive, we still get many calls from individuals and agencies who don't know what to do and where to turn." It was Jackie's turn to do what Elsa had done for her: encourage them when they were discouraged and connect them with the maze of the service system. Calls came in because the Jackie, who had received Elsa's gifts of care and encouragement, had discovered her own gifts of administration and encouragement and gladly shared them.

"Jackie . . . ," her driver called from the doorway, then pointed at her watch. "The roast . . ."

Jackie nodded, but it was in response to a faceless hurting human being on the other end of the line.

Jackie had been just another unknown, isolated person whom Elsa and Henry had sought out and taken the time to listen to one winter night. The invitation to visit Belmont Methodist Church that had fluttered through her mail slot nearly forty years ago had been the gift of care she needed to begin her march toward independence and real living. Now it was her turn to share that gift.

EPILOGUE

Jackie Page is program coordinator for Nashville's Disability Information Office. She plans to work until age seventy with twenty-five years of service. Her employment allows her to hire a full-time aide and live at home rather than in a nursing home. Jackie is considering publishing an autobiography. ❖

Jamie

HOW DO I LOOK, MAMA?"

"Oh Jamie, you look wonderful," exclaimed his mother. "Turn around and let me see your hunting outfit."

Eight-year-old Jamie was going on his first overnight hunting trip with his daddy, his grandfather, eight other men, and his twelve-year-old cousin David. Several of the other mothers helping Reba set up tables and chairs for the elementary school annual fall festival stopped what they were doing to inspect Jamie's new outfit.

"Those look like new boots," someone said.

Jamie beamed and held out his foot with its tan lace-up work boot for closer examination. Reba felt her heart swell with pride. He was a good-natured little boy who loved to be with adults. Reba resisted the urge to button his new denim jacket or to brush the wisp of brown hair out of his eyes. Instead she gave him a quick hug and said, "I'll see you Sunday, Jamie. I hope you and David get a squirrel."

Jamie's eyes sparkled with excitement. The men wouldn't be doing much hunting this trip—they would just be setting up camp. But Jamie's dad had promised that he and David could do a little squirrel hunting.

"Bye, Mama," he called.

THEY HAD A GOOD LIFE. Reba's husband, Bo, had worked with Reba's dad, Luther Harris, at the coal mines outside of Varney, West Virginia. Later, Bo drove his own coal truck. Varney is a town with no store and no stoplight; so small that it isn't considered a community, just an area. It is a region where local lore abounds, where coal is king, and where the legendary feuding Hatfields and McCoys once lived.

Reba, a petite brunette, had known Bo since she was fifteen, when her father introduced them. Bo hadn't swept her off her feet, but over time his soft-spoken, gentle sincerity and deep love had won her. She had addressed high school graduation invitations one week and gotten married the next.

Reba and Bo were a good match. Ten years her senior, Bo was a hardworking, deeply religious young man, with eyes that danced when he was happy, which was most of the time. Following a honeymoon to Carter Cave, Kentucky, they had moved next door to Reba's parents. The homes of relatives dotted either side of the road.

Five generations of family welcomed Jamie, Reba and Bo's first-born son, into this tightly knit cocoon of rural familiarity. Gina's birth a year later made their family complete.

SUNDAY BO CAME HOME FROM THE HUNTING TRIP WITHOUT JAMIE and unloaded his gear in their garage.

"Your dad wanted to work some more on his tree stand, and Jamie and David didn't get a squirrel, so I told him it was okay to stay," he told Reba who ran to greet him.

"Oh, okay. I know Jamie is having a blast," Reba said. She knew that her father would supervise Jamie well.

On Monday, Reba drove her cousin and her sick baby to the doctor. As they returned home, she noticed that the church parking lot next door to her parents' house was filled with cars. "I wonder what's going on?" she called to her cousin as they hurried to her mother's back door.

As they stepped in the door, she saw her suitcase. *What is going on*, she wondered. Inside somber looking family members had gathered. Her younger sister Karen came toward her. "There's been an accident," she said quietly.

Reba knew it had something to do with the hunting trip. Her eyes flickered over her waiting relatives.

"You need to stay calm," Karen said soothingly. "Jamie has been shot."

Reba stared at Karen in horror, "Is he alive?"

"As far as we know."

"Where was he shot?" Reba was trembling now.

"In the head." Karen was reaching for her, and her mother was suddenly at her side.

Reba thought of Jamie—his sweet little boy face with the pug nose. She remembered his smile on Friday; he was so proud of his new hunting boots.

"Who would want to shoot my baby?"

WHILE REBA WAS AT HOME, LEARNING OF JAMIE'S INJURY, her Uncle Eddie and brother-in-law Barry had gone to tell Bo and to bring him home. In his own mind, Bo had to believe Jamie would be okay. Even so, he began to cry. By the time Bo arrived home, Reba was sitting on the couch sobbing and clinging to Jamie's tattered teddy bear. The only news from Reba's father was that Jamie was still alive and at a rural hospital. Doctors were making plans to fly him to Charleston.

Reba insisted that the family call Jamie's pediatrician. As the family prepared to leave for Charleston, the pediatrician called back to tell them that he had spoken with a friend who was the head neurosurgeon at the Charleston hospital. "He'll take care of Jamie as a personal favor. They'll be ready for him when he gets there," the pediatrician promised.

The rhythm of the windshield wipers kept pace with Reba's thoughts as she tried to make sense of the accident and talked to God. God had given them this son and had protected him all this time. She couldn't understand the Lord's taking him away: *I know you have work for him to do, and he's only a little boy. He hasn't even begun to live or to do work for God. I know God has special things for Jamie to do.*

JUST A FEW HOURS EARLIER, JAMIE HAD BEEN SINGING and goofing off on the mountain, hoping to find a squirrel. Grandpa Luther laughed to himself, realizing Jamie would never get a squirrel while making that much noise. He let the youngster continue because enjoying the day was all that mattered. The snap and crunch of undergrowth signaled Kenny and David's return from the other side of the mountain. As they approached, a deer bounded past. "Did you see that?" Jamie and David shouted to each other, jumping up and down in excitement.

When David and Kenny were just four feet away from Jamie and his grandpa, David turned. His finger must have brushed the trigger of his shotgun, although it is hard to say what happened. The safety had been on. The gun fired. The blast immediately threw Jamie backward to the ground. Stunned, Luther picked up his unconscious grandson and quickly applied pressure to his bleeding head wound with an old cloth.

The minutes ticked by as the family raced the mile to the Bronco they'd driven up the deserted mountain. Kenny drove while Luther held Jamie. David rode silently in the back. *If anyone has to be taken, take me,* Luther prayed. Kenny looked down to see the speedometer reach seventy; he looked up as the Bronco careened off the road and over the side of the mountain. Miraculously, no one was injured, but the truck had slammed into a tree and was totaled. Luther, still holding Jamie, and Kenny and David climbed back to the road where a woman in a station wagon stopped to offer assistance. "There's a doctor's office in town. I'll take you there."

When Luther laid Jamie on the examining table, it was clear that he was in serious trouble. "Get the ambulance over here," the doctor ordered his receptionist. He then started Jamie on oxygen and wrapped a clean bandage over the head wound.

Once Jamie was loaded, Luther climbed in the ambulance. His grandson had not regained consciousness, and the color was gone from Jamie's face. At the hospital, the emergency room doctor peeled back the bandage and shook his head. "There's no way we can help him. Let's get a Life Flight down here from Charleston." They began transfusions and kept him breathing. That was all they could do.

The ambulance transported Jamie and Grandpa Luther to the airport, where they awaited the Life Flight helicopter. Approaching rainstorms kept the helicopter from landing. "Should we go on to Charleston or go back to the hospital?" the ambulance crew debated.

A pilot working nearby offered to take Jamie to Charleston in his small private plane. The ambulance crew quickly pulled the seats out to make room.

"There's no room for you in the plane," the crew told Luther.

"I can get into the tail," he pleaded as the plane was gassed. The pilot agreed. "But only if you promise not to move, no matter what."

PARKER FERGUSON, an old family friend, pastored a United Methodist church in Charleston. As the plane taxied for takeoff, one of Reba's sisters was alerting him of the accident. When Luther arrived at the hospital, Parker was there to comfort him and to wait with him until his family arrived.

"I've called my church," Parker told Luther. "Everyone is praying for Jamie and for your families. I'm here to help any way I can."

In the meantime, Reba and Bo had arrived with their family at the other major Charleston hospital. "He's not here," a receptionist told them after checking her records twice. The delay was maddening after the two-hour ride from Varney.

"I'll try to locate him," she offered. In a few moments she told them, "He's in surgery at Charleston Area Medical Center."

"Surgery?" It was another shock. They had not realized that he would be operated on so soon. Finally they entered the medical center where even more family had arrived. Tears, apologies, and self-blame flowed, but Reba and Bo were firm. It was an accident. They did not blame anyone.

After ten hours of surgery to remove the bullet and repair the damaged area of Jamie's brain, a doctor came to talk with the family. "Jamie is in extremely critical condition," he told them. "But he made it through surgery, which was a miracle."

BEFORE THE FAMILY SAW JAMIE FOR THE FIRST TIME, nurses tried to prepare them for how he would look. This preparation lessened the shock of seeing the massive bandaging around his head, the tubes in his nose and mouth, and the IVs in both hands. Doctors warned the family that if Jamie survived, he might never speak; he might have confused speech; or he might not wake up ever.

As each day brought difficult news, and Jamie remained in a coma, the family had the comfort of friends to refresh their spirits. Parker and his wife, Ethel, opened their house to Reba and Bo. A hot meal awaited them in the evening. Aunt Ruby and Uncle Roger had left their roomy van with Reba and Bo for their use during the day. Just to leave the hospital and be alone with their thoughts for a while helped. Bo's boss and wife came to visit.

"Do you need money?" she asked.

Bo didn't know what to say. "I can always use money," he replied. He had good insurance, but he was beginning to feel the pinch of meals, gas, and parking. She handed him several folded bills.

Five days after the accident, Bo and Reba agreed they would go home and visit with Gina, find someone to drive Bo's coal truck, and pick up fresh clothing. Jamie, still comatose, was having a hard time. His whole body was tensing. He held both arms tightly against his chest and drew up his legs, chewing on the tubes in his mouth and setting off alarms. It hurt to see him hooked up to machines and struggling so.

GINA HAD HER OWN STRUGGLES AT HOME. Reba's Aunt Jane, who lived nearby, was keeping the seven year old. Young children often regress behaviorally when terrible things happen, acting out their anxiety and confusion. They need a nurturing and reassuring environment to stabilize their behavior. Reba and Bo wanted and needed to spend some time with Gina to reassure her and to explain what the doctors were doing for her brother.

Gina wanted answers to her questions, "When are you coming home? When will Jamie come home? Will Jamie die? What does he look like? Can I see him?"

The answers to her many questions came in one response, "We just have to pray and trust God to bring Jamie through this."

To Reba and Bo, it seemed that everyone knew just what to say and do. Their family pictures had arrived at the portrait studio. Reba, afraid they would never have another family portrait, and yet too upset to go alone, called a high school friend to go with her to select a pose. NANCY picked her up, then sat and listened as she cried and poured out her story. Gina's teacher was also understanding. "It doesn't matter how much school she misses. You need her with you when you're home. I'll help her catch up her work." And she did.

DURING THOSE FIRST TWO WEEKS, BO, REBA, or her parents waited in the hospital's intensive care waiting room. The hospital nurses had attached Jamie's well-loved, beige teddy bear to his arm with bandages. On the tenth day Jamie opened his eyes and pulled the bear close to his face. That same day the doctors released Jamie to a semi-private room across from the nurses' station and took him off the respirator. The nurses removed the tubes from his head; only an IV and a feeding tube remained.

The nurses encouraged the family to touch and hold Jamie. His eyes were open, but he remained still and silent throughout the long days. The hospital staff suggested the use of tape recordings to stimulate Jamie. Cards, flowers, and balloons poured in, visible reminders of the love that surrounded them as doctors weaned Jamie from morphine and phenobarbital. The future was uncertain, but the friendships were sure.

KENNY and CARLA, friends of the family, visited on Halloween. Carla and Reba leaned over Jamie's bed, one on each side. They talked and teased Jamie. Reba had on a pair of earrings that Jamie loved: a spider on one earring, a spider web on the other.

"What is that, a snowflake earring?" Carla asked. Jamie laughed. It was his first reaction. His face lit up; his mouth and eyes smiled, but that was all. He couldn't hold his head up or use his arms and legs. He had no control of his motor abilities.

As the days passed, Jamie's right arm grew stronger. His head stabilized somewhat, and he could turn it from side to side a little.

"Jamie, it's wonderful to see you waking up," one of his nurses told him, feeding him pieces of chocolate chip cookie. Still Jamie did not speak. While Bo sat nearby, Reba sang to Jamie, "If I were a pig, I'd praise you, Lord . . . " Jamie grunted like a pig, but no one picked up on it.

That night, Bo stretched out on Jamie's bed and listened while Reba rocked their son in the rocking chair and sang. Reba sang the song again, "If I were a pig, I'd praise you, Lord . . ."

"Oink."

Reba stopped rocking. "Jamie, what did you say?"

"Oink!" he repeated a little stronger and louder. When Bo heard that little voice, he jumped up from the bed and knelt down by Jamie and Reba.

"Can you say daddy?" Reba asked through her tears.

"Daddy," Jamie repeated. Then he said it really loud: "Daddy!" Now the whole family was weeping.

"Mommy," he wailed. Word spread quickly though the pediatric wing that Jamie had wakened. Smiling nurses, brushing back tears of joy, rushed to see him. The nurses wanted to hear him talk, so they asked him to name each one of them. And he did.

"We've got to let my folks know," Reba said, reaching for the phone. It was a joyful moment she needed to share.

The family had gone to a school festival, and Reba called them there. "Find my dad and tell him that everything is fine and that I need to talk to him," she told the girl who answered. Luther, with family and friends trailing after him, ran for the telephone. Jamie wanted to talk to everyone, to tell them that he loved them.

The next day Gina arrived for her first visit with her brother. *How little she looks*, Bo reflected as she shyly entered the room. *This is hard for her too.*

"Jamie, you look like a bald-headed old man," she said, climbing up on his bed. He laughed but was not one bit offended. He wanted to know all about school and then asked for his school work. "I don't want to get behind."

Jamie grew stronger, but doctors wouldn't say when they thought he would be strong enough to go home. Reba laid across Jamie's bed as he awoke from a nap.

"What do you want to talk about this morning?" she asked.

"I want to talk about God. God came to see me last night."

Bo came over to the bed. "Where did you see God?"

"At the foot of my bed."

"How do you know it was God?"

"He told me it was God."

"What did God look like?"

"A real bright light."

This was too much for Reba, "Did God say anything else?"

"Yeah, God told me he was making me well."

JAMIE DID NOT KNOW THAT HE COULD NOT WALK. His behavior was babyish—he'd outgrown kissing people years ago but now was kissing everyone. And he wore diapers without raising any questions. He believed that the IV was holding him in bed, and Bo and Reba did not go into detail about his condition because they were unsure how much Jamie would understand. He made trips to the gift shop in a little wooden hospital wagon with tall sides and soft pillows. Custodians at the hospital dropped by Jamie's room with little gifts. His many cards, strung on ribbons, went from the ceiling to the floor. The nurses played with him. One made a sign that said, "Kisses for $1" and taped it to a urine specimen bottle. The atmosphere was appealing and filled with love and hope.

"Here, Jamie, use your fork on those eggs." Reba encouraged Jamie during their third week at the hospital. Jamie tried to grip the fork but then flung it on the floor. Reba picked up the fork, wiped it off, and handed it back to him. Jamie was angry, and he threw the fork to the floor again.

Jamie's behavior shocked Reba and Bo. It did not reflect the type of child Jamie had been. *He's becoming spoiled*, they thought and talked it over with the nurses. The nurses suggested that Reba refuse to feed him. Jamie refused to feed himself. When lunch came, Reba told him, "Either feed yourself or don't eat." Jamie didn't eat dinner either. When breakfast came, Jamie fed himself every bite.

This process was only the beginning of their learning how to work with Jamie. Sometimes a head injury will affect personality and behavior. A patient's response to authority may be passive-aggressive. Jamie may have felt that he could control something in his life through his refusal. Thus he did not eat. Jamie also refused to wear a necessary eye patch. He cried and cried.

"I won't take it off," the nurse told them. "If I do, he'll know that all he has to do to get his way is to cry."

Outside in the hall, one of the nurses took Bo and Reba aside. "Please don't make an invalid out of him. Treat him as you would a normal child. Don't treat him like anything is wrong with him."

Having others stand back and objectively tell them not to treat him as a disabled person was a necessary step in the process of getting well. In future years, that bit of advice would come back to Reba or Bo whenever they began to think, *Jamie isn't like the other kids; he can't go anywhere he wants to go.* And yet they knew that feeling sorry for him would destroy him and undermine his self-confidence. They'd have to learn to balance—and to remember Gina's need for time. They would have to remind others through the years that "Jamie can do that," or "Please, don't do that for him. It may take him longer, but he needs the practice."

Reba and Bo had so many things to learn. As the doctors planned for Jamie's discharge seven weeks after the accident, Jamie was still totally dependent on others. He could not walk, dress himself, bathe, go to the bathroom, or even sit up alone. He needed someone with him twenty-four hours a day.

THE NEWS OF JAMIE'S HOMECOMING thrilled family and friends. "He's doing better every day," they said, believing that one day Jamie would be the same little boy they had always known.

But Reba understood that she had no idea how to teach Jamie all the things that he could no longer do. And she knew that Jamie was not going to be fine. The physical therapist at their local hospital was pregnant and wouldn't be working much longer. Their rural area had no speech or occupational therapist or psychologist, and those were all professionals that Jamie desperately needed. The wheelchair they borrowed was not suited to Jamie's needs, but they realized that it would work for a short period of time.

As the months passed, Reba was the only one in her family capable of looking at Jamie realistically. He had limited use of his right arm and no use of his left arm. His legs refused to move, and they had to strap his head to the back of his wheelchair to stabilize it. To bathe him, Reba laid him in the tub and placed rolled-up towels on either side of his neck to keep his head from flopping from side to side.

Reba finally told her family, "I'm pursuing a rehabilitation facility for Jamie. And I'll go alone if I have to." Reba had requested information from various rehabilitation centers and felt that Rebound in Gallatin, Tennessee, held the most promise.

With new found support from Bo to investigate rehabilitation, together they prepared to visit Nashville and the facility. Reba's sister recalled Dan Forbes, a minister who had visited their church and who lived in the Gallatin/Nashville area.

"You might not remember me. I'm Barbara and Luke's daughter," Reba said when Jill Forbes answered the phone. Reba explained Jamie's injury. "My parents will be coming with us, and I wondered if you could save the Sunday newspaper? Bo will be looking for a job if we decide to place Jamie in Rebound."

"Please, stay with us," invited the minister's wife. Jill and Dan had a spacious home; all six of their children were grown and lived elsewhere. Dan and Jill welcomed them to Nashville. Then Dan accompanied the family to Rebound for Jamie's evaluation. The meeting raised everyone's hopes—they liked the facility and the specialists were aware of Jamie's many needs, validating Reba's observations. They spent the afternoon learning about the types of therapy the staff could offer Jamie, and they met patients who were making progress after devastating head injuries.

"I'm convinced they can help Jamie," Reba said as they left.

Bo nodded his agreement.

WITH JAMIE'S ACCEPTANCE FOR REHABILITATION AT REBOUND, Reba and Bo faced the move to Nashville, a city almost five hours from their home. It was a shock to think of leaving the lifelong support of family and friends. They would be terribly alone, but Jamie's needs came first. Dan and Jill had invited them to stay at their house until Bo got a job. So with fresh hope and lots of tears, Bo and Reba loaded their car, put Jamie into the backseat, and said good-bye to Gina. Having Gina stay with Reba's parents would provide stability for a time.

It was important to Reba and Bo that Gina have as normal a childhood as possible and that she continue to have appropriate childhood experiences and peer relationships. Barbara and Luther offered the gift of caring for Gina in the surroundings of family and friends.

The atmosphere was gloomy as more than twenty people stood in Reba's parents' yard to say good-bye. It was scary. Bo was tense. He was leaving his job and was already homesick. "I'm a fellow that doesn't like change," he had said hundreds of times.

DAN and JILL'S greeting of the Staffords in Nashville was a wonderful relief in the midst of being uprooted while barely coping with each day. The next morning, Bo and Reba took Jamie to Rebound. *Jamie will learn so many things at Rebound*, Bo and Reba reminded themselves as Jamie played with the computer at the facility. He would learn to cut up his own food, to transfer from a wheelchair to a bathtub, to get in and out of a car, to dress himself. Jamie would learn skills that would make him independent.

"It's time for you to go," a therapist told them. "It will be better if you just slip out."

Reba's heart sank. Jamie had been distraught when he learned that they couldn't stay with him. She worried that he would feel they had abandoned him. With misgivings, they stepped onto the elevator. As the door was closing, they knew Jamie had missed them.

"Mommy! Don't leave me in this place alone!" he screamed.

BO FOUND WORK AS A CASUAL LABORER AT FIRST. He had hired someone to drive his truck at home, and a bookkeeper had taken over Reba's part in their small trucking business. Their insurance premiums had jumped to $300 a month for Jamie alone, with a new deductible of $3,000 per year. Gas expense for the fifty-mile round trip to visit Jamie—daily at first, meals out, new clothing for Jamie, hand held shower hose, a $3,000 wheelchair, weights for his arms and legs, a standing box, a padded bench to work out on—all added expense to the base cost of Jamie's therapy. They had been debt free when they moved to Nashville.

Other struggles developed: The occupational therapist wanted Jamie's shoes tied; the physical therapist wanted them untied. It took months to see improvement in some areas. Everyone felt the stress and frustration that was building.

"Get counseling," staff members at Rebound advised them. They did. Bo and Reba had always talked honestly, but the counselor helped them face and work through the anger, resentment, disappointment, guilt, and fears that had built up. They learned that it was okay and normal to feel the way they felt.

Reba and Bo had always depended on their families to help them gain a better perspective. Now they were separated by long distances. Dan and Jill had invited the couple to remain at their home. It was a time of genuine need, which they believed God was leading them to meet. "Use our phone," Dan and Jill invited. "Use it whenever you want, we'll take care of the bills."

Family and friends consistently called Bo and Reba too, which helped to keep the expense of communicating down. Some nights the couple cried themselves to sleep; other times they were more stable, rejoicing in small gains. Barbara and Luther often brought Gina to visit on weekends, and having family there to talk about all that was happening helped keep things in balance.

Dan and Jill helped in other practical ways too. Dan helped Bo create a resume when he realized that Jamie would be at Rebound longer than initially expected. Jill was an excellent cook, and Bo and Reba learned to love her hot Cajun food. Without Gina and their normal routines and friendships, Reba and Bo often had too much time to think and worry. Dan and Jill took them to movies and concerts. They took them sightseeing and out for dinner. These breaks in the routine helped Bo and Reba see that life was going on as usual. They learned to laugh again. And of course, Jamie was the recipient of T-shirts, games, toys, stuffed animals, and books from family and friends in West Virginia. But the best gift Jamie received was his parents' ability to relax with him because others were stepping in with support.

Jill, who was always open to helping others, found that Reba and Bo's struggle strengthened her own faith. Despite their situation, Reba and Bo held steadfastly to their belief in God. The Life Fellowship Church that Dan pastored welcomed Reba and Bo. The members began to look for needs they could meet while praying for the whole Stafford family as it struggled to adjust to Nashville and the world of disability.

REBOUND WAS GOOD FOR JAMIE. The staff eventually requested that Bo and Reba visit once a week and later allowed Jamie to return home on the weekends. Reba worked to learn all she could about Jamie's care. She learned how to stretch and exercise him, learned what he could do on his own, and learned what to avoid. And she learned the magic that a dedicated musician could work while he moved Jamie toward a fuller range of motion.

NEIL LAFFELY was a young and enthusiastic music therapist. One afternoon as Reba arrived early to take Jamie home, the lilt of boyish laughter coming from Neil's music therapy room attracted her attention. With a pang, she realized the laughter sounded like her son's—in the old days. She stopped at the door and peeked in. The small room was filled with musical instruments. Neil sat in the center, strumming his guitar and singing. Without missing a beat, Neil presented a cymbal to his patient to strike at the appropriate time and then continued the song. When he finished, his eyes met Reba's.

"C'mon in," he invited, turning Jamie's wheelchair around.

"Jamie!" Reba said, her sadness lifting. Neil grinned.

"Music is a powerful tool. We're working on the neglect in Jamie's arm. We'll show you."

Carefully Jamie picked up the drum stick in his weak hand. By playing rhythm instruments or striking a cymbal on cue, he strengthened his arms.

"Can we play 'Blue Suede Shoes' again?" Jamie pleaded. Neil, with empathy and humor, was restoring the joy to Jamie's life.

AFTER SEVEN MONTHS OF THERAPY AT REBOUND, the staff released Jamie. During his stay, Jamie had finished second grade with the help of a tutor, regained control of his head, and could almost push himself up out of his chair. He'd even learned to stand by keeping his feet apart and bracing his hands on his knees.

Once it had become clear that Jamie would benefit from long-term rehabilitation, Gina joined Bo and Reba in Nashville. Bo found an excellent job as a truck driver, and Reba worked in Dan's business. They enrolled Jamie and Gina in a local elementary school, and Jamie began outpatient physical therapy three times a week at a nearby Nashville hospital. While there, Jamie learned to use a sports wheelchair—a lightweight, easy-to-manipulate model. He also learned to stand with the aid of a walker. But the resignation of two of his therapists left Bo and Reba searching for a new rehabilitation center.

"Can you recommend something to keep Jamie moving forward with progress on his arm?" Reba asked Neil. She feared that without therapy Jamie would stop working and would lose the strength he'd gained.

Neil had admired the family's spiritual strength and decided to give his talents to the family free of charge, once a week. He couldn't imagine anything worse for a parent than a child's being injured. And yet, this family was teaching him to see the bright side of even that— that there is hope. He had seen so many families split apart by head injury. This family not only survived but managed to be thankful for everything. The Staffords were a unit, and that was a wonderful thing for Neil to experience. He missed his own family members, who were strong and close also. To spend time with another strong family unit was energizing. He was giving and receiving.

Neil always considered the head-injured person to be a new person. "He or she will never be the same old person ever again," he often said. At first, families and friends think the person will get better; they want the old person back. When that doesn't happen, old friends disappear. Then the family and the survivor are left alone. He tried to educate people that the survivors still have needs. Friends and family must rediscover them as new persons who want to lead a normal life; persons who want to go out and be with people and not be stared at. Neil also understood the importance of encouraging head injured persons to do things for themselves instead of putting them into a helpless role. Doing things by themselves gives dignity and self-respect. "Allow the struggle," he told families. "Learning is taking place."

Neil taught Gina to play the flute and Jamie to play the drums. Bo learned to play the trumpet. Neil taught them to read music and gave them pointers on different instruments, but the major focus was getting Jamie to use his arm. Low motivation often accompanies head injury. Group therapy with his sister and friends had the advantage of peer pressure—Jamie could showcase what he was doing and receive praise for it.

Neil became part of the Staffords' life for a time and continued to be friends always. It was nice to work with someone and not have to charge them and to stay as long as he wanted. Neil also grew in his respect for Jamie as the boy practiced without complaint.

"He's amazing," Neil told Jamie's parents. "He still has a strong belief in life."

JEFF MARVEL knew Reba, Bo, and the family through the church. Jeff had always tried to find ways to minister to people's needs. "That's my lifestyle," he explained to Reba and Bo one night as they talked about Jamie's lack of progress. "I can't help the whole world, but I can help the part of the world the Lord put me in." As a rehabilitation coordinator at an insurance company, Jeff was in a position to network with a group of physicians.

Jeff knew Jamie and liked him. He could see that the family was losing hope and having a rehabilitation plan would help. Jeff also knew that family members without a medical background or a rehabilitation background accept the information that neurosurgeons or specialty surgical groups give. The neurosurgeons and surgical group members have a different outlook than a physiatrist, a specialist in physical rehabilitation, which is a new field within the last decade.

"A neurosurgeon does all he or she can and then moves on," Jeff explained after church one morning. "It's important to get to people who specialize in rehabilitation care." Some of Jamie's physicians were giving bleak outlooks, saying, "If he's gotten 50% better and it took three years, it may take five years to get 10% better than that."

"We're not ready to accept that Jamie has come as far as he can," Bo told Jeff. "But where do we go from here? These professionals should know best." Jeff's knowledge and ability to connect them with professionals in the rehabilitation area gave the Staffords new hope. Jeff knew the Staffords had an excellent support system, better than most he'd ever seen. They would be available to help Jamie with massive amounts of therapy if prescribed.

SO MANY HANDS WERE WILLING that Jamie got the help he needed to make solid gains. With biofeedback and electrical stimulation at a Chattanooga, Tennessee rehabilitation center, it was clear that Jamie did have isolated movement in all areas of his legs and arms. With years of therapy, he could gain more use of his limbs. Persons from the church quickly volunteered to help Jamie.

Jamie's new doctors stressed physical goals—learning to fish again, to go hunting and camping—plus an understanding of what it would take to reach those goals. Then the work began.

Through countless hours of therapy, Jamie regained full shoulder movement, a good amount of elbow movement, and a minimum amount of wrist and finger motion. His legs strengthened for standing and his trunk muscles became very strong.

Dan and Jill were often away for a month at a time on missionary trips, and Reba struggled to get Jamie up the stairs at their tri-level. He weighed almost as much as his mother. Reba and Bo had grown to love Nashville, so they decided to move into an apartment—the only one they found that accommodated a wheelchair in the bathroom.

When news of the planned move reached church members, many arrived to help. Reba loved the new apartment with its fresh paint and wallpaper borders, the porch swing in front, and a complex in which Jamie could get around in his wheelchair unassisted. When he did turn over in his chair, neighbors were glad to help him up.

JULIE and JEFF METTS met Reba and Bo at a church convention in Nashville. Julie and Jeff also had young kids and the couples became close quickly. The Metts family began to attend the Staffords' small church where the family's heavy physical therapy schedule was well known.

Bo felt closest to those people who were considerate. These persons understood and remembered that he and Reba were having problems they had never had before and that they were making decisions they had never dreamed they would have to make. Was Jamie working hard enough on his therapy? At what point did they quit and go back home? How were they to balance Jamie's extraordinary needs and Gina's? How did they keep family outings "normal" when everything was so abnormal?

Their sharing group at church had been studying the implications of being the body of Christ. Julie and Jeff had been struggling with their move from Michigan when they became friends with Reba and Bo who helped them talk through some family issues. To them it had been a continuous circle—one gets weak, the other pulls him or her up.

Julie grieved for Reba's struggle and Jamie's losses but she didn't know how to communicate her concern. She asked for God's help to "just be family." She expressed her need for guidance to appropriately assist Jamie. Jamie, who was now eleven, was able to tell her what to do.

One afternoon as the two women sat on the porch swing, Reba began to talk about her fears, "Perhaps I've done something wrong that caused God to punish us through Jamie." Julie could not let that go unchallenged, "I don't know a God like that. I only know a loving God. You weren't doing anything wrong. It was just something that happened. God didn't stop it. Maybe God did allow it to happen, but you cannot think that something bad is going to happen if you make a mistake. I believe God is aware of the whole picture—what looks horrible to me is not as bad as it seems, and God will reveal himself in it."

"That makes sense," said Reba. Just verbalizing this guilt was a reality check. Julie had pointed out the realities, putting Jamie's accident into perspective. As they talked, her private thoughts lost their power over her, and she became less obsessive in her brooding. Julie recognized the unhealthiness of letting her grief for Jamie's losses take over and looked for ways to give Reba and Bo some space.

Julie was honest. "I don't know what to do."

Reba reassured her new friend, "Just being there is such a help." Julie learned to ask the person in the situation directly what she could do to help. To save Reba some time, Julie would take Jamie to therapy. This concrete assistance provided the time and space with Jamie so that he began to open up to Julie.

As they became closer, Julie began to realize the impact of Jamie's disability—constant need for therapy and doctors' appointments, Bo's absence as he worked to earn a living, and Reba's natural preoccupation with getting Jamie's needs met. Julie began to understand that having someone who could spend time and focus just on Gina was a gift she could give. She would intentionally zero in on Gina's needs.

Jamie idolized Julie's husband, Jeff, a handsome businessman and pilot, who had his own airplane. Jeff often asked Jamie to go with him to his health club or took Jamie for a ride in his airplane. When the time came to begin the intensive physical therapy prescribed, Jeff offered to help. Jeff had never been around anyone in a wheelchair, and he felt clumsy and awkward. He didn't know what topics were safe to talk about. All he knew was that Jamie had been shot, a unique and strange situation.

Jamie's maturity surprised Jeff, although the boy often mumbled. Bo and Reba gave him advice, "Treat him like you would anyone else." So Jeff mumbled back; Jamie laughed and began to speak up. As Jeff invited Jamie to go places, he began to see the ongoing struggle with a wheelchair. When he took Jamie to the bathroom, he realized the difficulty of getting Jamie in, getting himself in, and then getting both of them out with the chair.

It pleased Reba and Bo to have Jeff as a role model for Jamie. Jeff didn't treat Jamie as an invalid. And with Jeff and Julie's help, life was fun again; they were becoming a family again.

Bo believed that while you can't forget what's happened because you do have something to deal with, you have to strike a balance and remember the good things. "If I look at Jamie and start crying at what I see and remember what was, it's depressing to everybody," he explained to Jeff. "We have to build the atmosphere that surrounds our lives with a positive mental attitude."

Part of the attitude came from keeping both kids active. They learned about different activities for kids with disabilities and enrolled Jamie. Jeff offered to take Jamie to his therapeutic horseback riding lessons on a permanent basis, which freed Reba to spend time alone with Gina. Jamie took golf lessons from a golf pro in Nashville and became proficient. He was learning wheelchair tennis also.

Jeff and Julie's daughters were becoming close friends with Jamie and Gina. Jamie had been hesitant to make friends because he didn't want to be a burden to anyone. He knew he couldn't do the physical things other children his age could do. Gina was quite protective of her brother, getting sandwiches, toys, glasses of water, and anything else he wanted. Soon the Metts girls were telling Jamie, "Get it yourself" as they took Gina off to play with them. Before long, Jamie was caring for his own needs.

In the midst of Jamie's tragedy, Bo and Reba were discovering a new life. They were learning that family is more than relatives. They were forming close ties with this new community. They not only were surviving; they were thriving.

Jamie often stayed at the Siskin Rehabilitation Center in Chattanooga for several weeks at a time for intensive physical therapy. Two boys from the church, JOSH and NICK, came to Siskin to visit and to spend the night with Jamie. Most rehabilitation centers have an activity room; and the boys played Nintendo, table tennis, and watched movies on the VCR.

Josh's parents, BARRY and KATHLEEN, helped their son know what to do and what not to do by talking with Reba and Bo. They asked about some of the details of the accident and what Jamie was comfortable talking about. "How does he like to be helped getting around in his wheelchair? What about bathroom trips—exactly what kind of help does he need, and how much can he do on his own?" The next time Josh and Nick visited, Bo suggested that they try out the wheelchair and move around the apartment, so they could understand what Jamie had to do to maneuver. Soon everyone was laughing as the boys ran into walls and furniture.

Barry had always believed that God loves a cheerful giver; when God has opened your eyes to a situation, it's time to help. Look, see, and do your part. Barry knew Bo worked odd hours. His own steady schedule with two jobs limited the amount of time he could give, but when Dan and Jill circulated a list of people to help with therapy, Barry signed up for certain nights. While Reba did activities with Gina, Barry kept Jamie at his exercises, making it interesting by counting slowly or teasing him.

Often Josh invited Jamie to spend the night at his house. At first, Jamie's getting out and doing things on his own scared Bo and Reba. The boys also wanted to shop and go to the movies on their own. After talking it over, the parents agreed they could handle it. These types of friendships allowed Jamie to develop as a normal twelve year old.

AS JAMIE'S REHABILITATION CONTINUED, Jeff Marvel witnessed the excitement in the entire Stafford family that Jamie could improve his physical condition. The family and the church experienced renewed enthusiasm and renewed hope. Jeff knew that peace came for the family and the patient only when they know they have done everything they can do to get better. Siskin Rehabilitation Center and the church community gave Jamie the opportunity to be the best he could be. It also let the family members know that they had done all they could do. Then they could find a place of contentment and resolution.

The church community tried to maintain a positive outlook without putting inappropriate pressure or unrealistic expectations on Jamie. The locus of control remained with the family and with Jamie, where it belonged. Jeff believed that the best environment was for medical professionals and supportive friends to provide constant support for the family members, realizing that they are making decisions to the best of their ability.

When Jeff spoke to Reba and Bo about decisions, he did so in a loving, caring manner: "I have made these observations, and I feel or sense the following process might be good for Jamie. But I respect your decision and will support your decisions fully." Jeff felt that each person had gifts to offer, and each person needed to be allowed to give them. The main thing we have to communicate is a caring heart. We need to back up our words with actions. We may not know how to show care, but if we ask questions we can find ways. The key is to ask persons what their needs are.

KIM MARVEL often called and asked, "How are you doing?" Her response to Reba's "All right" was, "No. How are you *really* doing?" Kim was always available and willing to take the time required to hear what Reba needed to say. Reba knew that Kim was always willing to come over to the house to pray with her or to cry with her. Reba and Bo *appeared* to be handling their hectic schedules and the emotional stresses well. Kim acknowledged their feelings below the surface.

Kim also understood the effort involved in taking Jamie anywhere. She routinely called Reba prior to shopping. "I'm headed to the grocery store. Do you need anything?"

MARY also was willing. Mary was available even in the middle of the night. Bo's absence with his trucking company three nights a week created a void when the "Why did this happen to us" feelings plunged Reba into deep depression. A mother and father weren't next door and a sister wasn't up the street to help Reba sort through the agonizing pain she sometimes felt.

Mary worked at Vanderbilt University in Nashville and worshiped with Reba and Bo but lived some distance away. When Reba learned that Mary drove all the way home before the evening church service, she invited her to stay in town with her family on those nights. As they shared what was going on in their lives, Reba learned that Mary had arrived in Nashville with just fifty cents in her pocket. She had found a minimum-wage job to which she had walked and had subsisted on beans and oats for long periods of time. "I washed my clothes in the bathtub and did without television," Mary laughed.

"But you survived," Reba said. Mary became a solid listener.

"What do I do with his life?" Reba wondered aloud.

"Reba, you have to deal with what is happening to Jamie now, not with what is going to happen in the future. Right now you must prepare him for life in a wheelchair. It doesn't mean you have to give up hope—just be realistic."

By allowing Reba to bounce ideas off her, Mary helped Reba explore options. Mary also acted when she heard a need. When Reba's grandfather died, she told Mary, "Jamie and Gina have been through so much trauma. I hate for them to go through any more. But I want to go home to Varney for the funeral. . . ."

"Let me stay with them," Mary offered.

Other times Mary simply called to share scripture or to talk. She had a gift of being able to listen and to understand what a person was really saying, to discover their real hurts and needs. To Mary, talking was therapeutic. To understand more clearly she sometimes said, "I think I hear you saying that Jamie's therapy schedule is too heavy for you to handle. Is that right?"

Mary also reminded Reba of what God had already done and of the successes and strengths Mary had witnessed in Reba. "You are surviving this. Jamie is making progress. You are exhibiting a lot of courage in not accepting and blindly believing Jamie's prognosis." Mary admired Reba's loving and godly way of relating to her children—no ultimatums just firmness and love. Mary let Reba know that she was learning from her.

"I've shared your story," Mary told her. "It is amazing to watch how God provides for you and incredible to watch it all work so well." Mary knew the Staffords' support group was dedicated to discerning the will of God and then doing it.

JUDITH and WAYNE arrived in Nashville five years after Jamie's accident. Judith had prayed for deeper relationships; in Nashville, she found true depth through the Staffords and those who surrounded them. They attended Bo and Reba's church. Their nine-year-old son, Nathan, looked up to Jamie, and the two boys discovered a common interest—computers. Kim and Jeff had loaned Jamie one they weren't using.

Judith and her family enjoyed the outdoors and often encouraged the Staffords to picnic with them at a community park where they could fish off the banks. As their relationship deepened, Judith was struck by Reba's openness. If a need arose, Reba would call Judith. Judith could see how well Jamie's therapy worked with a small group and looked for other ways to help.

"We can make some meals," Judith offered. She and Wayne knew Jamie needed contact with people. They spent time counseling with Jamie rather than doing the physical therapy. They knew Jamie needed people who would listen without judgment. Judith also talked with Bo and Reba about meeting Gina's needs.

As the families spent time together, Judith began to see Jamie's need for autonomy despite his physical dependency. Judith's gift would be finding ways for Jamie to be independent—allowing him to be alone with a friend at the mall at a movie, taking more responsibility for his own therapy, claiming time for himself, speaking up for himself and his own needs.

The next year Jamie stood up for himself when therapy got to be too much. Instead of becoming angry and withdrawn, he was able to tell the adults in his life, "I don't have any time for myself. I understand I need to do therapy once and maybe twice a day. But three times a day, along with schoolwork and occupational therapy and biofeedback, is too much. I need time for myself."

Reba agreed. She had learned from Julie and Judith to look out for Jamie's total well-being—physical, emotional, mental, and spiritual. Together they worked out a new plan that satisfied Jamie.

SIX YEARS AFTER THE MOVE TO NASHVILLE BO AND REBA AGREED that it was time to move back home. They had left Varney, West Virginia, a frightened young couple searching for the services that would give their son his quality of life back.

We've come full circle, Reba reflected. She stood at the door of her parents' home and watched Gina and a cousin rig up a pulley to a sled to get Jamie up the side of their mountain. The three were building a cabin in the woods.

The little community of Varney offered Jamie a freedom that he did not have in Nashville. Just last week Jamie wheeled himself to his cousin Matthew's house up the road to spend the night. Later he'd decided to come home in the dark to take a shower, flying down their rural road, going the speed fourteen-year-old boys go when no one is looking. A neighbor, hearing a loud crash, had picked him up out of the ditch while another neighbor came to tell her, "I think he's going to need stitches." She drove a sheepish Jamie to the emergency room. "I wish they would hurry," Jamie fretted. He was anxious to get home and on to Matthew's.

Jamie was learning to drive a four-wheeler, and only a few days ago his dad had taken him hunting. He'd finally gotten that squirrel. Reba was learning to let go of her fears to let him experience the things he wanted to experience.

"Mama," Jamie hollered from the back of the lot. She stepped outside to see what new thing he had to show her. She knew that Jamie and the family would have to face many new things, both obstacles and joys. She thought of her Nashville friends. The neurosurgeons' skilled hands had saved Jamie, but their church community's gentle touch had given his life back to him.

EPILOGUE

Jamie, fifteen, is now 5' 7" and weighs 130 pounds. He still uses a wheelchair for mobility. Part of his physical therapy comes from his standing to work on the engine of the 1966 Nova that he and his Uncle Larry are restoring. Jamie did get a four-wheel vehicle and insists that anyone who rides it wear a regulation helmet. Gina, now fourteen, is busy baby-sitting. Bo is operating heavy machinery in the coal mines once again. Reba fills her days with teaching since she home schools both Jamie and Gina. Together, the family is renovating a home across the road from Reba's parents' home to make it wheelchair accessible.

The Staffords stay in touch with many of the members of their Nashville church and visit whenever they can. ❖

Jim

THE SCORE STOOD AT 28 TO 26 WHEN KAREN GOT THE BALL, dribbled to half court, and flicked off a pass to Kelli.

"Guard them," shouted Bobby. "If they get off another shot, it's hopeless."

The referee rolled his eyes as two of Bobby's players moved in to guard Karen. She could control a game; and when her school had walked away with the state high school regional championship, Karen, not surprisingly, was named All-Regional player. Her classmates used adjectives like *happy*, *selfless*, and *funny* to describe her. Her quick laugh and easygoing nature drew people to her.

On the other hand, Bill, captain of the opposing team, was intense but reckless. When a play came together spontaneously, he was quick with praise and strong pats on the back. Bill was the emotional player on the floor. He tended toward the dramatic with a pass behind the back or a sky hook from impossible distances.

The referee knew that as the final minute ticked away, Bill would be the one to watch. If Bill got the ball, chances were he'd fake a shot and then pass off to Mandi, the youngest member of his team.

Kelli shot the ball back to Karen, and the gym fell silent except for the echo of the ball as Karen dribbled down the golden oak floor. The referee kept his eyes glued to Karen, watching as Bill entered his field of vision. Expertly, Bill reached in and flicked the ball from Karen, straight into Mandi's waiting hands. *Click*. Mandi raced unguarded for the basket, and as the final second ticked away, dropped in an easy lay up.

Click. Click.

"You saw it, didn't you?" grinned Karen.

Click. Jim made an excellent referee.

Kelli turned to Mandi, "Your basket doesn't count. Dad fouled me getting the ball away. We win. Again. Don't we, Jim?"

The referee clicked one more time to signal yes.

"Thanks, son," said Karen.

"Yeah, thanks, son," joked Bill.

"I can't believe we lost to your Mom . . . again," Bobby said, winking at Jim. Jim smiled broadly. He always refereed the basketball games that the Williams and Shannon families played.

BOBBY WILLIAMS AND HIS FAMILY WERE NEW FRIENDS of the Shannon family. They attended the same church, and often the families walked together on the high school track.

"How's it going?" Bill had asked Bobby one evening as they fell in step together at the track. Soon they were deep in conversation, each sharing about his own family. From those conversations, Bobby learned more about Bill and Karen's son, Jim. When he had first seen Jim at church Bobby had wondered, *How do you get to know somebody when they can't talk?* Talking with Jim's dad gave him useful information. Bill was glad to explain that Jim knew and understood everything that was said although he could not move or talk.

"He can respond with a click of the tongue, which means yes. When he sticks out his tongue, that means no."

"That's easy enough to remember," Bobby said.

"He's really a neat kid," Bill told his new friend. "He just doesn't want to be left out."

Bobby began to go out of his way to include Jim in conversations and to invite Bill and Jim to visit or eat supper when Karen took Kelli and Mandi out of town. He and Bill began to eat lunch one or two times a week and to visit on the phone—casual conversation, just checking in. He followed Bill's lead and talked to Jim like the nineteen-year-old man he was. When Bobby told a story or a joke, he always included Jim.

Both of their oldest daughters played high school basketball. Bobby noticed Bill and Jim sitting on one of the corners of the basketball court. He'd realized that Jim could not move his head. The corner seating gave him a view of the entire floor, but it also isolated the family from the other fans. Jim and Bill couldn't get into the bleachers because of Jim's wheelchair, so Bobby joined them on the floor.

Bobby came from a small family—and having the Shannons as part of his extended family was a wonderful bonus. He and his family got to know the Shannons well. They learned that Kelli was serious and studious and would give any of her belongings away to a friend. Both families celebrated when she received a full-tuition scholarship to college. Bobby soon realized the truth in Mandi's words, "My friends' moms are always out. My mom, Karen, is always at home." He learned that Mandi was very sociable—always talking on the phone and going out with friends. Both Kelli and Mandi played the piano, took dance and voice, and played basketball. They had participated in numerous plays and talent shows and were very involved in church work, camps, and school clubs.

And Bobby and his family discovered that Jim was a whole lot smarter than most people and a lot funnier and more caring. You just had to get to know him. But in the beginning, all Bobby knew was that Bill was a veterinarian, and Jim couldn't move or talk.

KAREN DAVIS AND BILL SHANNON SEEMED DESTINED TO MEET, fall in love, and marry. Both were outgoing and popular, and both shared a passion for basketball.

Following high school, both attended David Lipscomb University in Nashville where Karen finished with a degree in education. After his first two years at the school, Bill transferred to the University of Tennessee. He then went on to Auburn University in Alabama and earned a degree in veterinary science. Bill's sense of humor, warm caring nature, and love of children had attracted Karen. When she'd asked, "Why vet school?" he'd replied, "I'm just too compassionate to deal with hurt people."

After college graduation, Karen taught a year of elementary school and found it to her liking. She and Bill planned to remain in Hendersonville and married in their home church surrounded by lifelong friends. Bill launched his veterinary practice and Karen taught two more years before their first child, Jim, was born.

Jim's birth was normal. The score doctors assign newborns for strength and alertness was high. Karen and Bill did not notice anything wrong until Jim was between six and nine months old. While their friends' babies were sitting up, Jim was not. By nine months the young couple watched as their tiny, light-haired baby held things and did a fair amount of crawling around their new home, waiting for him to sit. The day Karen saw him stand up in bed, she felt her heart leap. He stood up in bed only once.

At nine months Jim's pediatrician ran tests and called Bill with the results. The doctor conveyed a lot of information, but the words *general category of cerebral palsy* struck Bill so hard that his breath began coming in short gasps.

"Will he be able to walk?"

"Well, he can't even sit up. Why would you expect him to walk?" the doctor said tersely.

The moment of diagnosis carves itself on the heart of every parent, because that moment breaks the parent's heart. Twenty years later, Bill still could describe in excruciating detail the words and the setting of Jim's diagnosis. For both Bill and Karen, the hardest part was accepting. For years they struggled to help their son and to make sense of this tragedy.

Elise H. Wentworth writes about the day of diagnosis in her book *Listen to Your Heart*:

> That sunshine-filled life you had envisioned has disappeared, and now you feel that you can see only a dark wilderness ahead; you are afraid because of the strangeness. You do not want to believe it is true, and yet you must. Your happiness and your child's happiness depend upon how well you accept him [or her] as he [or she] is. . . .
>
> Now at this beginning, you stand at one of the major crossroads in your life. Which of the two diverging paths you decide to follow is your choice, for although others may advise you, the decision is yours alone to make. Neither path is smooth, yet the one that is marked Rejection leads to the dark gloom of despair while the other path leading to Acceptance will carry you to that destination which is the ultimate goal—good adjustment.

Karen and Bill had decided to be involved in Jim's development every step of the way. While Jim was between the ages of two and three, they frequently made the four-hour trip to Memphis for his therapy. At Les Passe, a development center for children who are not walking, they received training in how to teach others to "pattern" Jim. Experts then believed that the crawling experience was related to later reading ability. The program required the patterning seven days a week, three times a day. The counselors suggested that Karen train people rather than do the patterning herself.

The task of finding at least sixty volunteers did not daunt Karen. She went to her pastor at Hendersonville Church of Christ and explained that she needed volunteers to help with Jim. The volunteers didn't need to know anything special; she would provide training, and she only needed an hour of their time per week. The volunteers could bring their children.

Through a verbal announcement in church and a sign-up sheet, Karen received the names of seventy-five women, and the program began. Some had worshiped with Karen and Bill; others had wanted to help but had not known how to approach Karen. Working in a group made it easy.

Jim, now a gregarious three year old with brown hair and huge green eyes, lay face down on a special table designed and built by Karen's father. One volunteer stood at each side and one at his head. They moved his arms and legs in unison in a crawling motion and turned his head from side to side on a counted exercise that lasted thirty minutes. It was hard work. Jim's impish personality entranced the volunteers, and they encouraged others to join them.

Karen enjoyed having the women get to know her son. They were discovering what she and Bill already knew: he had a sweet disposition and was fun to be with. He smiled at the women and talked to them a little. It wasn't long before they were relating to him as just a little boy.

Having volunteers do the patterning, freed Karen to do chores or to spend time with Kelli, who was born three years after Jim. At the end of the hour, the volunteers left with the feeling that they were doing something important and worthwhile.

Often Karen baked something and took time to visit after the women finished the patterning. She made the volunteers feel like part of her family. Soon everyone began to look forward to seeing their new found friends.

NAN BATEY, a church member, immediately volunteered. She knew that an individual's emotional situation affects everyone. The outcome can be positive, or the individual can become bitter. The invitation into Karen and Bill's home showed Nan the love Jim's parents had for him.

"I know it is difficult for you to receive," Nan told Karen one day. "But thank you for allowing us to come and help." Nan felt fortunate to work with a family so warm and loving. As a parent, Nan could easily imagine the struggle of these young parents. She wanted, through her actions, to reassure and to encourage them that others really cared. Nan believed everyone needed to be remembered and cared about.

When Jim was four, his therapists realized that the patterning was not making any difference, and the family chose to discontinue it. However, through that time of close personal contact, people became attached to Jim and his family. They relished his successes as well as the successes of Jim's sisters, Mandi and Kelli. It was hard to say what that physical touch meant to Jim, but as he grew older he became a self-confident individual with a good sense of humor, well connected and well loved by the church members.

Jim had even figured out what to do about all those little kids, and not so little kids, who stared at him in stores—smile. It made all the difference in the world. Along the way, he'd learned that success was not measuring his bag of marbles against someone else's bag of marbles. Jim measured success in the way each person learned to deal with the life he or she had been given.

BETWEEN THE AGES OF FIVE AND SIX, DOCTORS at Vanderbilt evaluated Jim for probable cause. They found none and gave no prognosis.

By the age of seven, Jim could barely speak and could not hold things physically. His head control had always been poor and since that time, he had no control over his arms and legs or any part of his body other than his chin.

Jim's day evolved as he grew up but has always consisted of four meals a day. He writes the following on his computer, using specially designed technology:

A normal meal, unless I'm really tired, usually takes around three quarters of an hour. When I get really tired, my entire body, including my mouth, goes kaput and I can't eat a thing. I mostly eat sandwiches, fish, chicken, fruit, chips, dairy products, lasagna and ground beef. I have a major sweet tooth. The only vegetable I'll eat is a potato. Any type of a potato except boiled. On occasion, we have steak and Mom will grind the meat because I can't chew it. My favorite meal is breakfast. The only things I don't like about breakfast are eggs and grits. I get choked very easily. When allergy season comes around, it's especially difficult for me to eat. I am a very, very, very, very, very messy eater and use lots of paper towels. In my life, I bet I have used a ton of paper.

Jim has been mainstreamed into the local public schools since kindergarten and has learned at the same pace as his classmates. Cerebral palsy has not impaired his ability to learn.

Jim typically attends school, writes letters, works on his computer, watches television, and studies. Karen gets Jim up and has him fed and dressed and ready to go to class in seventy minutes.

It takes forty to forty-five minutes to give Jim a bath from the time he is undressed until he is back in the chair with his hair washed and fully dressed. A bathroom renovation created a walk-in shower with a gently sloping floor, which allows easy access to a newly purchased bath chair on rollers.

Expense is the consideration of any renovation that makes life smoother. The shower chair cost $1300. Besides redoing the bathroom, other costs include a big van and a lift, plus the cost to ramp the house and widen all the doors. Communication devices are the only way Jim can communicate with the world, but Medicaid recently declined to pay for his communication devices. Bill and Karen's insurance didn't pay either.

Opportunities abound for churches and individuals to pool their talents to build needed ramps, to provide renovations, or to supply funds for needed equipment for persons who require them.

"WE'RE GOING TO MYRTLE BEACH THIS YEAR," Bill Shannon mentioned to LINDA KEMP at his veterinary clinic. "We thought it would be fun if you and Terry brought Leslie and Kellen and came with us."

Linda had worked with Bill for several years, and she enjoyed visiting with Karen. She taught swimming and lifeguard training in the summer, and she loved the water. "A trip to the ocean sounds wonderful," she said.

At the time, both Jim and Leslie were four years old and Kellen was seven. The children had grown up together, and occasionally Linda and Karen traded baby-sitting duty. The Kemps knew the Shannons never let Jim's disability keep them from enjoying life. At the amusement parks, Jim went on all the rides with someone holding onto him. At the miniature golf courses, Jim played with someone holding the putter with him. Through her work with Bill Shannon and their joint vacations, it was clear to Linda that caring for Jim was very time consuming. She felt that it was important to relieve them occasionally. She could do that in South Carolina and at home.

"Let me keep Jim sometime," she'd offered at first.

Karen had been doubtful. "He chokes a lot," she explained.

"I know first aid, and I teach lifesaving so I know what to do when someone is choking," Linda told Karen. "I'd like to keep him sometime. Maybe we could trade off every once in a while, and you could keep Leslie while I run errands."

That appealed to Karen, and she agreed.

THE HOUSE THE SHANNONS HAD RENTED was across the road from Myrtle Beach. It had four bedrooms and a screened-in porch that faced the ocean.

"This works well," said Karen, as she and Linda shared dinner preparation. "What about our keeping Leslie and Kellen one night while you go out, then your keeping Jim and Kelli while we go?"

"It sounds perfect."

The next morning the two families awoke to the roar of the surf and kids chasing Frisbees. "We'll catch up with you in a little bit," Karen said to the Kemps while spooning up another bit of cereal for Jim. "Breakfast takes us a little longer."

Linda looked around. Jim had a wheelchair, a float, and a beach umbrella to haul to the beach as well as the assorted blankets, books, and cooler that got everyone set for the day.

"Let us help with this stuff," suggested Terry. "When you come down to the beach with Jim, we'll be all set up."

The week rushed by. Jim floated on the ocean with Bill or with Leslie and her dad. Jim played in the sand, sitting between someone's legs with a sand shovel held in his hands. It was also a week of learning for the Kemps.

"Karen, you're up every night. Is everything okay?" Linda asked one morning.

"Oh, that's because I have to turn Jim every two hours."

"Every night?"

"Yes."

At the week's close, the families promised they'd do it again. And they did. The routine stayed the same, but Karen learned to ask "Is everything accessible?" As Jim and his wheelchairs got heavier, having a ramp to wheel him down to the beach made it so much simpler.

KAREN AND BILL WOULD HAVE WELCOMED THE INVOLVEMENT of more children with Jim—to come and play games or cards with him. Jim often won board games when the family sat down to play. People who have taken the time to get to know Jim have discovered that he loves football, basketball, the Bulls, Michael Jordan, and listening to tapes.

Despite his parents' concern about the lack of child friends, Jim grew into a person who didn't wait around for people to come visiting. He kept an active schedule, attending church and Sunday school and carrying a regular course load in school. He began using a computer in second grade and by attaching a headset, Jim is able to use his chin to interact with his computer. His computer can serve as a communication link with the community.

Jim first built sentences one letter at a time. With improved technology, he now can select a word from a list of words on his computer screen, switch screens, choose another word, and so on as he builds sentences. He also has the option of making himself heard through the use of his voice synthesizer.

Jim's computer allowed him to do his own outreach. After new people visited the church, they received a personal letter of welcome from Jim—a lifelong member. He developed the letter, which included some information about himself and some about the church, and had the preacher approve it. Each time someone joined, he printed a copy and had it mailed. Jim made it easy for new people to feel at home in their new church and to get acquainted with him.

"So you're the one who wrote that wonderful letter to my son," the new preacher said when Bill introduced him to Jim. "I would like to thank you for writing him." Jim was sharing a welcome. And since the preacher's son also had a disability, it was an opening for Karen and Bill to share the best way to access services and programs in this new location.

At church, Jim had triumphs and struggles. Jim's Sunday school teacher told him what the next week's lesson would cover. That way, Jim could read it at home. When it was time for class discussion, Jim could add his insights through the use of either written notes or later, answer with his voice synthesizer. The struggles were often physical. The church had no elevator, and it was difficult to carry Jim up the stairs to Sunday school.

Part of Karen's outreach involved steering people in the right direction for their legal rights, sharing how to get school programs, and educating persons as to their disabled children's rights. Currently she serves on the board of the TAC (Technology Access Center), a communication and technology access center with the expertise to help individuals decide which communication device works best for them. The center can supply the available technology to help persons with disabilities access their environment. The center has switches that turn lights, televisions, and other appliances off and on; electric doors; lifts; and anything that promotes independent living. It not only evaluates needs for persons with disabilities in the school, home, or workplace; it also suggest where to purchase the necessary items.

"C'mon Jim!"

Jim couldn't help but see the group—Mandi, Kelli, and Leslie floating on their rafts—watching for his arrival on the beach. High school would be coming to an end in a couple of years, and the Shannons and Kemps were back at Myrtle Beach for a week.

Karen carried the two rafts while Bill struggled to lift Jim from his chair and carry him to the water. Karen tried to steady Jim's raft so his dad could get him onto it. Suddenly six sets of hands were holding the raft still.

"These waves are *the* best!" Mandi gasped, then shivered. "I'm going back out."

Their little group floated lazily from wave to wave—lulled into a deep restfulness by the warmth of the sun, the salve of sun block, the dark glasses shading the eyes. Then it struck. From out of nowhere, a giant wave soundlessly dropped upon them. Leslie felt herself pushed down by the force of the monster wave; she came up spitting salt water.

"Jim!" she hollered, but all she saw was her bright red float racing for shore. "Jim!" she yelled again, eyes straining for Jim and Bill. Riders on floats bobbed everywhere but no Jim.

"Leslie," Bill called from thirty feet away. Bill and Jim had been knocked off and swept away by the wave, but the rope that Bill always tied around Jim's waist had kept them together.

"Are you okay?" Leslie asked automatically. The huge grin on Jim's face told her that he was having a great time.

Click, said Jim as Bill wiped saltwater out of his son's eyes and hoisted him back onto the float. For Bill, spending time with Jim was fun. If anyone had asked him that day, he would have said, "Jim's no trouble. He's a joy. He just doesn't want to be left out. You've got to look ahead instead of looking back."

Jim was relaxing again, floating between his longtime friend and his dad. He wanted to tell all the kids in wheelchairs, "Don't be passive; don't be afraid to be adventurous."

At Jim's pool at home, Leslie had watched as Jim's dad took him underwater and dived off the board with Jim on his back so Jim could have that experience. She'd watched his family treat him in an ordinary manner, and she treated him the same way. She'd learned how to converse with Jim. Often they talked about her basketball season.

"I bet you're dying to know how many points I made."

Click.

"Twenty six."

He'd reply in the negative by sticking out his tongue.

"Oh, no way you say. Okay, you're right, twelve points."

Click.

JIM LOVED PHYSICAL ACTIVITY and when the opportunity came along for him to try horseback riding, he took it. Jim writes on his computer:

The Tex Ritter horseback riding program was on Monday nights at 7:30 P.M. in a big shed. I rode with a pretty high school senior, a basketball player named Alyson Amonette. She was extremely smart. While we were on the horse, she told me about herself, about her family, about her future plans; sometimes she told me about her problems. Each week I wrote a note on my computer for Alyson that had a little crazy comment or a question for her. I couldn't wait for Monday night because besides church and school, that was the only contact I had with people my age. By the end of the program, I could hold my head up like it was second nature. In my opinion, the program not only helped me physically; it also helped Alyson mentally and emotionally.

BECKI PETRICK, a licensed therapeutic riding instructor for the program, told Bill and Karen, "Riding improves balance, coordination, self-esteem; loosens tight muscles and tightens loose muscles. Jim is very tight, but when he rides his muscles will relax. There is probably no other therapy that can do that. A horse's hips are similar to a human's hips. When someone like Jim who does not walk is forced into a centered seat, he experiences a motion that moves his hips and relaxes his muscles."

Becki loved her work for this organization sponsored by United Cerebral Palsy. It was open to all riders with a disability, if there was room. Volunteers and equipment were always in short supply. The Sumner County 4-H Club staffed Jim's program as a citizenship project. The club also supplied some of the horses. Entire families of 4-H members had bonded with these new riders. They were discovering the joy an evening a week brought to kids who never dreamed they could get out of their wheelchairs and ride a horse.

"Kids are just kids," Becki had told the volunteers. "They want to laugh and have fun." Volunteers take home a smile: they've made someone's day, and it improves their day too.

The program is simple. Volunteers attend a two-hour training session, then work at leading horses. Riders, depending on their disability, play games such as "red light, green light" or starting and stopping the horse on command. All the games teach control of the horse, while improving the rider's balance.

Not only was the riding therapeutic for kids and adults with disabilities, but the setting provided an opportunity for parents to exchange information. They talked with parents who had older children. They could learn about their achievements. They could look into the future and see their child accomplishing some of those same things.

This poem by John Anthony Davies explains what therapeutic riding can mean and why volunteers can make such a difference.

I Saw a Child

I saw a child who couldn't walk
sit on a horse, laugh and talk.
Then ride it through a field of daisies
and yet he could not walk unaided.
I saw a child, no legs below,
sit on a horse, and make it go
through woods of green
and places he'd never been
to sit and stare,
except from a chair.

I saw a child who could only crawl
mount a horse and sit up tall.
Put it through degrees and paces
and laugh at the wonder in our faces.
I saw a child born into strife,
Take up and hold the reins of life
and that same child was heard to say,
Thank God for showing me the way.

Because Jim could not balance or grip the reins or saddle, Alyson, an experienced rider, served as a backrider for him. She put one arm around his waist and used the opposite hand to hold Jim's head steady.

At first, both Alyson and Jim were nervous. But after two classes, Alyson looked forward to coming. She realized that while Jim was nonverbal, a lot was going on in his head. *I'm going to know the individual in that body*, Alyson thought.

The way Jim lived his life amazed Alyson. She decided to become a research doctor to find a cure for people with cerebral palsy or for a cousin's deafness. As the riding course continued, she realized that Jim would rather have respect for who he is. She didn't have to feel sorry for him. That respect allowed her to come to know Jim as a seventeen-year-old computer whiz and to forget about his disability. Alyson wrote the following on her college entrance essay:

> Jim and I created a bond of friendship that will never be replaced. As soon as he is wheeled into the barn, he is looking for me and I for him. Together, we have learned more about horses and about relationships with other people. The therapy that I give once a week does not come from experience. It is based on kindness and understanding, and it works. My week begins each Monday night in a dark, cold barn. But it is a barn full of love, and it makes me look forward to the dreaded Monday.
>
> It was not like we were on a horse, it was like walking around and talking. His determination and struggle to get it perfect was inspiring. Once I learned how to communicate, we had conversations, and I phrased questions so he could answer yes or no. We talked about colleges and about what we were doing in school.

EDUCATION WOULD BE JIM'S TICKET TO A FUTURE he could enjoy. It would give him the opportunity to make some choices about his life as an adult. A paper on self-determination by the National Information Center for Children and Youth with Handicaps says: "People with disabilities have diverse needs and abilities. . . . Most people with disabilities have this in common: they can express their own viewpoints, and can make informed decisions about matters that affect every aspect of their lives." School gave Jim a chance to be with his peers, to form relationships, to increase his knowledge, and to participate in social activities.

As Jim's senior year in high school approached, Karen admitted, "I think we need to slow this down a little. I just can't keep up." Jim agreed. He would take an extra year to finish. No one knew better than he the number of hours his mom put in daily, reading his textbook assignments to him and helping him complete his school work.

Jim enjoyed high school. Classmates treated him like he was just a "normal punk kid" and built his self-confidence. He writes, "I am satisfied with the kind of life God has given me. Don't feel sorry for me because I'm in a wheelchair. Just because I am in a wheelchair, it doesn't mean I am stupid, deaf, or don't have feelings. I like to go to a ball game, go to a good movie with friends, or play a game of gin rummy just like any other person."

As his class prepared for graduation, the members included Jim. The entire Beech Senior Class of '89 signed the class picture and presented it to Jim during a school assembly. His senior classmates voted Jim "most intellectual."

Things were winding down at school, and Leslie was finishing up her senior year of basketball. Life was exciting as the high school girls' basketball team headed for the state championships. If possible, Jim attended all of the girls' games each year. Even when the gym was virtually empty, Jim and his mom or dad were always there rooting for them. As the girls huddled, Leslie said to her teammates, "Jim's been our most faithful fan. Don't you think we ought to dedicate these games to him?" No one had thought of it, but everyone wanted to do it. Leslie was recognizing Jim's gifts of support to her team. Jim was quickly rolled out on the floor, and each player gave him a high five as she ran out. Later he was photographed as Beech's number one fan.

THE LAST MONTHS OF SCHOOL ALSO RAISED THE ISSUE of the senior prom. For a long time, Jim had been thinking of asking Leslie to escort him. He wrote a letter to Leslie and left it at the school office that day. When she was called to the office to pick up his letter she opened it and read, "Dear Leslie, Would you please honor me by pushing me in the senior walk?" Jim's request surprised Leslie. It hadn't occurred to her to ask him. She responded, "I would be very honored." The night was one made for memories. Jim wrote,

A few days before the prom, I went to a tux renting place. My favorite color, other than the color of money, is blue. I got a black tux with a blue tie and cummerbund. The day of the prom, Leslie brought a pink rose to Dad's clinic for me to put on my lapel. That day I hardly ate a thing. Dad brought the tux and rose home around 4 P.M. I got dressed and when I looked in the mirror, I said to myself, *Darn, I'm handsome. Look out Tom Cruise, here comes James Stanton Shannon.*

I had been waiting on Leslie about ten minutes, when I saw a vision of loveliness walking up the stairs. It was Leslie. I thought, *Holy moly.* I have never seen any female more beautiful than Leslie was that moment. She was wearing a pink off-the-shoulder hooped dress and a single strand of pearls on her perfectly tanned neck. That night will be a night I'll never, never, never, never forget.

Jim had lots of fun with Leslie. They'd gone Christmas shopping together a few months earlier, and for the first time no one in his family knew what he'd bought. Jim had invited her to concerts. They'd sat in restaurants after her tennis matches and visited with friends while sharing a soft drink. Every time she took a sip of her drink, she picked up Jim's glass and gave him a drink too. When she didn't understand what he wanted to look at in the music store, she simply went through the list, "Is it country? Is it rock? Is it jazz? Is it religious?"

Click.

"Okay, here we are. Now, is it Amy Grant? Is it . . . "

WHEN THE MINISTER AT HENDERSONVILLE CHURCH OF CHRIST suggested that the Wednesday night men's class consider a series entitled "Struggling," class members identified issues they could relate to: the loss of a child, having a child with a disability, the death of a spouse, divorce. Class members asked Bill if he would talk to them about what it was like to have a child with a disability. Bill agreed.

What can I tell them? Bill wondered as he sat down to make some notes. He had stored some of his memories away; some he had never shared with anyone. Perhaps someone in the class would have a child or a grandchild born with a disability or who would become disabled through an accident or illness. Bill decided the best thing he could do was to be painfully honest. Here is what he shared with the class:

I am happy to share with you my personal struggle in raising a child with special needs. It's going to be hard for me to openly discuss some very personal situations, but I'll do my best and try to get through this. You'll have to bear with me.

Yes, it has been a struggle. Have you ever had your heart ripped out and just thrown on the floor? Well, seventeen years ago, I did; and my wife did. And it's been seventeen years putting it back in. The words on the other end of the phone cut right through me: *Your son has brain damage, motor function disparagement.* The voice went on and on, saying something about a block in the red nuclei; then, "we'll have to lump him into the general category of cerebral palsy."

My response was, "Will he ever be able to walk?" That was about all I could ask I was in such a state of shock. The doctor's answer was cold, "Well, he can't even sit up, why would you expect him to walk?"

That began the toughest time of my life. Let me stop here and tell you Jim's situation. He has cerebral palsy. He is considered a nonverbal, that is nontalking. He is a quadriplegic, which means he can't use his hands, arms, legs, or feet in any sort of a functional capacity. But he does have a mind, and that is the best thing. He can see and hear well. His motor functions are just compromised. He is extremely bright. He goes to regular school, Beech High School, and is nineteenth in his class of 256 students. He is happy most of the time and seems to have fewer problems with his disability than we do. He just wants to be included. He will surprise you—he looks like a child, but he is so smart it is startling.

Those early years were the worst for me. The initial shocks were overwhelming. I remember the day I talked to the doctor over the telephone. My dad stopped by my office with someone for me to meet. I took Dad outside and walked about and started crying and told him what I'd learned. You know when you were young and had a problem or were in trouble, you could talk to Dad and he would take care of it. But this time, Dad couldn't take care of it.

I remember he put his arm around me and said, "We'll work it out the best we can." But all I knew was that this was real and the problem was mine. It just hit me in the face like a brick.

This began the endless stream of trying this doctor and that, this hospital and that, this method of therapy, et cetera. We couldn't leave one straw unturned that would help our son walk and talk. There was swimming, patterning exercises that the women came and helped with—and equipment, computers, speech therapy; trips to Nashville, to Memphis, to all cerebral palsy centers—most of which did little or no good. But I must tell you, any little bit of improvement that he achieved felt like walking on the moon.

We pioneered nearly everything that worked. You can't just go somewhere and have it all programmed out for you. There in the first years, what I call the shock years, that was the worst time of struggle. I really quit living for a while. I didn't care if I lived or died. It took about a year or so for the inner me to come out of that depression. I know Satan used that opportunity to come into my life. I sinned. I cursed God. Oh, I went through the motions of being a good guy, but I wasn't and I confess that to you before God right now. I even tried to drown my sorrow with liquor, and I took the Lord's name in vain and did many things I am ashamed of. I tell you this because I think it is vital for you to know the agony I went through.

What is it like for a parent to have a hurt child? Those things I did against God have been a burden on my back all these years, even today. I have prayed about it a lot, but somehow it won't get off my shoulders. I am afraid I may have set the wrong example and unknowingly led someone astray. Maybe this talk tonight is God's way of helping me to shed that guilt. Would you pray for me?

You can see so far that the struggle was within me. After getting past the shock years, I finally got "self" out of it and feeling sorry for self and put the real focus on my son, where it belonged. I struggled to help him have as normal a life as possible and have our family go on and live and stay together. Can you imagine the pressure of wondering if the second and third child would be normal? It was intense. Do you know that statistics show that most marriages break up with the father's leaving and the mother's taking care of the child? I saw the parents of my cousin who had cerebral palsy split up.

We as parents have had to, and still do, make sacrifices. Karen and I rarely get to go off to do things together. One has to stay home. That's just the way it is. Unless one of us is there to help him do everything, well he just sits and watches TV, and we can't accept that. I have taken him to church, ball games, trips, swimming—jumped off the board so he could see what it was

like, talked boy-talk to him that he missed because he did not
have a close boy friend.

Let me give you a schedule:

- ❖ Karen and Jim up at 6:30. She bathes, toilets him, feeds
  him. That takes one hour.
- ❖ I take him to school.
- ❖ I go to work, and Karen does all the work at home for a
  family of five—cooks, cleans, shops.
- ❖ She picks him up early at school, and he comes home for
  a two-hour rest.
- ❖ From 3:30–6:30 she studies with him and prepares
  supper.
- ❖ We eat supper. It takes Jim forty-five minutes to eat.
- ❖ I do the dishes and help the girls with their homework.
- ❖ Karen finishes up Jim's homework by 8 P.M. He goes to
  bed at 8:30.
- ❖ We spend time with the girls until 9:30 or so, and they go
  to bed.
- ❖ Then I get my time to relax, read, watch TV until 11:30.

All night Jim has to be turned every two hours. Karen turns him
half the time, and I turn him half the time. You know what is
better than money? To sleep the whole night through.

Our girls have been wonderful. They don't get all the time and
attention they need, but we try not to overdo him and leave them
out. It's always amazed me how they accepted the situation as
well as they have and never asked "Why?" like other kids have.

I want to share with you a main factor in my return to living
life as a Christian should. It is what I term, for lack of better ter-
minology, the quiet Christian. Many of you here tonight are responsible for what I am today. It wasn't some really biblically
educated or fluent preacher. It was you who gave me the direction I needed—not so much by direct teaching but by example. It
was the way you always came to church with your family, some
job you did for the church, something you said in Sunday school,
or a prayer, or at a neighborhood group that said, "I am a Christian; this does really matter." It is the Ed Edgins, Larry Grahams,
Glen Rodgers, Bob Lees, and Lee Willinghams, Mike Browns,
Harry Johnsons, Huston Hudsons, Jerry Robinsons, Collins
O'Briens, Don Litchfords; and especially two men who are gone

at an early age, Glenn Garrett and Bill Rice. Couldn't you see Christ in them? Didn't they help you through some of your personal struggles?

I had the privilege of talking with Bill Rice when he was first diagnosed with cancer, and I told him that he influenced me more for good than anybody I knew (and that happened before he got cancer). And do you know he and I had never had a conversation before that day. It was just Bill Rice being himself. It was his example.

It is a continuing struggle now to look ahead for my son. Financially—well, you know what costs are involved with the [disabled], the expensive wheelchairs, ramps, vans, lifts, medicines.

School. It's a problem to find a college within a reasonable distance to meet his needs. We struggle with, What after school? Will he be able to work, or get married, or live on his own? What happens after we are gone?

After college, our next step is to get a facility for total living going for those who are physically [disabled]. Jim's major struggle now is communication. We are working toward that goal now. With his inability to communicate, you don't know the real Jim Shannon, and that mind and soul is aching to reach out and touch you and be touched back.

Jim wants you to know he is not a kid anymore. If any of you want to learn more I would gladly show you. I know it's hard to get involved in more than just a superficial way, but if you do, you'll find it's worthwhile. My friend Don Helton has, and Jim worships him because he never leaves him out. He comes and watches football games, plays poker—even took Jim to a Dallas football game.

In summary, it has been a struggle—a struggle for seventeen years. It's been a time of the lowest lows and the highest highs. I know you can all attest to the highest point, which was the day Jim was baptized. And I know there is a reason for me to have a [disabled] son. And the reason Jim and I have made it this far is because of the church. And who is the church? It's you. Every one of you.

THE CLASS SAT IN STUNNED SILENCE FOR A MOMENT. Bill had given them a totally honest testimonial, wrenched from the heart. His words would mean different things to each person in the class. For one, a new understanding of the essence of life—the appreciation of small miracles through bits of improvement; to another, an understanding that when you feel like you've quit living it can be the body's way of giving time to the spirit for preparation; to someone else, it's okay and necessary to feel sorry for yourself at times; and to another, the strong realization that if you neglect yourself, you will have nothing to give eventually. The reality of the family's journey was excruciating.

How many opportunities to show love and care had persons missed through false assumptions?   Persons had let opportunities slip by without saying, "I'd like to get to know Jim better. Would you teach me how to communicate with him?" Or, "Gee, it must take a lot of time to feed Jim. If you don't think he'd object, I'd like to try it while you're at home. If it works for him and me, maybe I could do lunch while you walk around the block." Or, "There must be times when you'd like to go to one of the girl's activities and Jim would like to stay home. What type of training could I get to make you comfortable with my keeping him?"

After Bill's talk, one class member figured out where he could fit into the picture and went to the minister. "Why don't we raise money for Jim to go to college?"

"It sounds like a good idea. But please clear it with Bill first," the minister said.

When JERRY called, he said, "Bill, this is what I want to do." He described a nice meal for $100 a plate with proceeds to go to Jim's college fund.

"I appreciate it, but I really don't think it's necessary," Bill said.

"Bill, this isn't charity," the man continued. "It would allow people to participate and feel like they could help. Jim has done a lot of work. He's college material. Why not let others have the satisfaction of knowing he's in school?"

"To receive money is something I am not accustomed to. I'm used to working for money," Bill told Jerry.

The class member totally understood Bill's position but felt Jim's situation was extraordinary. As they talked, the man's sincerity won out, and Karen and Bill allowed the fund-raiser so others could express how they felt. To church members, it would be a fund-raiser where everyone felt good. No one would be coerced, and the fund-raiser would include the local community.

A small committee compiled a list of names, to which the Shannon family added. The committee assigned a table of ten each to ten individuals. They invited people to come. Invitations included an address for mail contributions for those who could not attend but wished to participate. A bank account was set up. The local newspapers did a feature story about Jim's life and his plans for college. They included information about the expense of a full-time aide, which added new understanding to the dilemmas that families with disabled college students face.

Jim and his family got caught up in the enthusiasm. Jim began to write his speech for the evening. He would use his voice synthesizer to "speak" to the crowd. RSVPs from friends around the U.S. came.

The event was a blessing to the church members as they shared their gifts in preparation for the dinner. They finally had a way to connect, not only to the Shannons, but to one another. The Shannon family knew it would be a night to remember when the local church jokesters called and asked for a variety of family pictures to make into slides for the program.

"What are you all planning?" asked Karen when they came by to pick them up.

"You'll love it. We promise," they assured her.

Jim had worked hard, and the committee members admired the whole family's accomplishments. They felt the best tribute would be a good-humored roast. Members talked to Karen and her parents and Bill's parents to get ideas for the show, focusing on Jim.

The enthusiasm mounted as preparations got underway. Friends from inside and outside the church worked together. Until Bill shared what his family faced day to day, many in the church were unaware of how much time and expense accompanied disability. Bill's open sharing developed an increased awareness within the congregation of what some families struggle with daily.

JIM, DRESSED IN A YELLOW SHIRT, BLUE AND YELLOW TIE, and dark slacks could feel the anticipation build as his dad pulled into the country club parking lot. Scores of people greeted them as they entered the dining room, and Jim happily smiled at friends from far and near.

The dining room had become a wonderland. Tall silver candleholders with cream-colored candles sat on the head table; servers in black trousers, starched white shirts, and black bow ties moved through hundreds of guests. Finely crafted flower arrangements donated by a church member sat on deep burgundy tablecloths.

Bill wheeled Jim to his place next to podium, then held Karen's chair for her. Mandi and Kelli in print church dresses sat at the opposite end of head table. The room was alive with conversation, as men in suits, women in festive dresses, and children in their Sunday best mingled. This was a party.

BILL WRIGHT, who would emcee the evening, was not surprised at the turnout or the enthusiasm. He remembered that many of the same people had been present almost fourteen years earlier at a Christmas party for people who had patterned Jim.

"What a marvelous dinner," minister Ken Dye said from the head table. "The idea came up when Bill Shannon gave a talk on struggling. Jim, we're here to honor you and your friends." Around the room sat individuals who had forged relationships with Jim and his family—church, school, and community friends. "Jim has something to say, and he will use his computer voice synthesizer. His message is also printed in your program if you would like to follow along."

All eyes were on Jim as Karen and Bill turned on the computer connected to his wheelchair and held the microphone to his synthesizer speaker. Some of those present would hear Jim's own thoughts spoken for the first time:

I must have many friends in Middle Tennessee because not many people would spend $100.00 to eat and listen to a computer talk. I love sports, especially basketball. My favorite team is the Beech High School Lady Buccaneers. I collect hats and silver coins.

I would like to thank all of you for coming tonight. I also would like to thank all of my aides for helping me through school. It does my heart good to know that there are men like Jerry Jarrett. A scholarship was a good idea. Thank you for caring about me.

Then the emcee took over. Bill Wright introduced local county commissioner Steve Botts, who informed the crowd,

> November 14, 1989, has been proclaimed Jim Shannon Day throughout all of Sumner County.
> We've come tonight to pay tribute to Jim Shannon, not because of his disability but because of his tremendous ability. Even without his special needs, Jim set a record in public schools of Sumner County that would deserve commendation—a 4.3 grade point average out of a 4.0, a member of the National Honor Society.
> James "Jim" Stanton Shannon
> Whereas Jim Shannon, a member of the 1990 graduating class of Beech Senior High School, excelled in his studies, ranking fifteenth in a class of 257 students,
> Whereas Jim was inducted into the National Honor Society,
> Whereas Jim's infectious smile has endeared him to the faculty and students at Beech High School and has won friends for him throughout Sumner County,
> Whereas Jim Shannon has been involved in numerous extracurricular activities and rarely misses important sporting events of the [Beech] Buccaneers,
> Now therefore, I Steve Botts, as chairman of the Sumner County Board of County Commissioners on this the 14th day of November 1989, proclaim this day to be Jim Shannon Day in all of Sumner County.

The planning committee had saved the humorous roast for last. MIKE BROWN joined Bill Wright at the microphone. Both wore matching blue polyester tuxedos. "You've been proclaimed and honored, but we are here to roast you a little," they announced. "There aren't many people we care enough about to come to a dinner that honors him," said Mike.

"In fact, there are very few people in this room who ever had a dinner to honor them," added Bill.

As they continued, the lights went out and a slide show began.

To tell your story, we go back to 1971 when you were born at a very early age. You've had help from a lot of people who love you. I remember when your family put the pool in. [*a picture of Jim and his dad*] You stayed in the pool so long you began to look like a seal. [*a glorious color shot of a very wet looking gray seal, then slides of Jim's winning a student of the week award at Beech*]

Mike read Jim's reflections on the event aloud: "The best award I ever won was Student of the Week. They announced it on the intercom and told me to come to the office to get my prizes—a long-stemmed red rose and two gift certificates. My English teacher gave me a box of my favorite candy."

"Jim, these slides tell part of the story of a very special young man whose community has come to pay special tribute to you. Life is not dependent on strong and healthy limbs. Life is from the mind, the heart, the spirit within. Your life has been full because of love. Love is a verb not a noun. Love comes to you from family, from friends, then flows back into the community. While you watch the slides of your life, listen to this song."

As music filled the room, the audience could see some of the many facets of Jim's life:

Jim in a ball cap . . . Jim with his sisters Kelli and Mandi . . . Jim in the Dallas Sky Dome . . . Jim with Leslie at the prom . . . Jim on a boat with friends . . . Jim at the beach . . . Jim on a carousel . . . Jim on a horse with Alyson . . . Jim with his church group . . . Jim with his Mom and Dad.

The fund-raiser was a huge success. Jim would be going to college and the financial load would be lighter. But the real gift that each person there received was the feeling of being part of the body of Christ through meaningful service, of being part of a community.

EPILOGUE

After graduating from high school in 1990, Jim continued his education and earned an associate degree in business and finance at Volunteer State Community College. The opportunity to attend classes connected him with two new aides—Rosetta, who shared Jim's outrageous sense of humor; and Mike, a former serviceman, who initially had dreaded his student assignment to help Jim with calculus. Both Rosetta and Mike have become Jim's personal friends. And as Mike said, "To know Jim is to know someone with inner strength. My perspective on disability has changed. I am more respectful and filled with admiration—it's intensified tenfold after working with Jim. I want to see him graduate from a four-year college and succeed."

Jim writes of his relationship with Mike: "Going to the movies with Mike was a first because I have never been anywhere without Mom and Dad. I had a blast. Mr. Mike is like a brother to me. I tell him stuff I don't tell anyone else. I've never had a friend like him."

Jim plans to continue his education, using the funds from the fund-raiser to attend either Middle Tennessee State University or Wright State University in Dayton, Ohio. He will pursue a degree that will allow him to use his computer and math skills.

Kelli has completed a semester of college work in Italy. Mandi has followed the family tradition and plays basketball as a sophomore at Hendersonville High School.

Karen and Bill have become powerful advocates for disability issues and persons with disabilities. Karen continues to serve on the Tennessee Access Center Board, creates floral arrangements for weddings, and is considering seeking a master's degree. Bill owns and operates his own veterinary clinic. ❖

Christina
& Natalie

OUTGOING AND VIVACIOUS, SUZIE and her seven-year-old daughter, Nikki, had been on their own for five years when she met Ralph Foster at an electronics company where she'd recently gone to work. For more than a year Suzie introduced Ralph to the California she had always known and loved. Ralph, an only child, was solid and responsible. He had moved across the country with a friend after graduating from Fairmont College in West Virginia. He had fallen in love with the rhythm of the ocean, the sailboats with their white canvas taut against the wind racing across crystal blue waters, the warm ocean breezes gently massaging mind and spirit, the nearby San Bernadino Mountains with breathtaking vistas of pine forests and powdery white ski trails. *This is home*, he decided as he began his career as an electrical engineer.

Suzie's friendship, their outings with Nikki, and dinners with her parents who lived nearby connected him to family once again. At a company party the two friends saw each other with different eyes, and their relationship became romantic. Ralph, realizing that Nikki made them a trio instead of a couple, chose to ask Nikki's father to allow him to become a permanent part of her life. With that agreement, Ralph felt free to ask Suzie to marry him. Six months later, Ralph and Suzie were flying to Ralph's hometown so his family could attend their wedding.

THE BIRTH OF THEIR BABY, CHRISTINA, a year later was a happy time for the whole family. Nikki was a great help, running for diapers and baby powder and searching for ways to be with her little sister. Nikki would shake Christina's rattle, tickle her feet, wind up musical toys—anything to get Christina to look at her and respond.

"Happy?" Ralph asked one evening, as they sat outdoors in the warm California night air.

"Umhmm," Suzie said, flashing him a warm smile. "All I've ever wanted was to be a mother and have babies and take care of them."

That year was filled with firsts for the dark-haired, dark-eyed baby who resembled her big sister in so many ways. The first time she grabbed a rattle and shook it; the first time she accidentally pushed herself onto her knees, wavered a bit, then rolled over and smiled; the first time her tiny fingers wrapped around a table leg, and she pulled to a standing position and looked to see who was watching.

Suzie, Ralph, and the girls could have been any California family. Their small starter home in Jurupa Hills closely resembled all the other light-colored stucco homes in their subdivision. Many of their neighbors were having babies too, and it was fun to take the girls out after supper. *She's growing*, Ralph mused, as Christina gripped the index fingers of their hands on her first walk to the corner.

"I'm going to Grandma's," Nikki called after them, running quickly up the street with her ponytail bobbing. It was great to have grandparents just a block away, especially with Ralph's folks across the country in West Virginia.

"What do you girls have planned for tomorrow?" he asked.

"It's hard to believe, but it's time for Christina's twelve-month checkup and her measles, mumps, and rubella shot," Suzie answered, giving Christina's fingers a little squeeze. Ralph grimaced.

THE SCREAMING BEGAN RIGHT AFTER CHRISTINA'S measles, mumps, and rubella shots; then came the seizures, her little body ramrod stiff and convulsing, then limp and barely breathing. The rush to the hospital was fraught with a terror that was softened only by the sure knowledge that the experts would fix whatever was wrong with Christina. The doctors probed and tested, shook their heads, and passed her along to a new specialist. All the wonderful milestones of Christina's first year disappeared as Suzie and Ralph searched for a diagnosis that did not come.

Christina's behavior—a period of normal development replaced by seizures and loss of acquired skills—was vastly different from anything the doctors had ever experienced. Suzie and Ralph found it hard to keep hoping that somehow Christina would get better when she continued to regress. Christina's twenty-word vocabulary vanished, replaced with crying and screeching. She threw herself to the ground in fits of shrill screaming; other times she bit at her arms or flapped her hands. Out of control, she would run through the house knocking over anything in her path, then want to be held and comforted. As Ralph rocked her late at night the what if's assailed them. What if they couldn't find the cause? What if they did, and it was too late? They had tried to control her with the usual discipline for youngsters, but she did not respond. Some friends became unsympathetic, hinting that Ralph and Suzie could do more to teach Christina. They were searching, but no one had any answers.

"MARRIAGE ENCOUNTER," EXPLAINED A COUPLE at Our Lady of Perpetual Help, the Catholic church Suzie and Ralph attended, "is a weekend retreat designed to make good marriages better." By now Suzie and Ralph had been searching for a diagnosis for almost two years. Desperate to give Ralph a normal, healthy child, Suzie had become pregnant and was expecting the baby in a few months. "Let's go," Suzie whispered enthusiastically.

The weekend opened up a whole community to the couple, people they had known casually and others they did not know at all. With so many negative reports on Christina, it was becoming clear that the experts believed she had a devastating condition from which she would not recover. Suzie believed that the openness of the people they met at Marriage Encounter was the most wonderful thing that could have happened to them.

MIKE HOPSON saw the Fosters at church once in a while with a beribboned Christina. Though he knew that the Fosters were searching for the reason for Christina's developmental delays, their lives seemed pretty perfect. He and his wife Pattie had met the Fosters at the Marriage Encounter weekend, but he had no idea of what they were really struggling with at home. How could anyone understand who has not known the panic that arose with each new behavior that signaled the wrongness of what was happening to Christina?

KATHIE and DAN NEFF had met Suzie through Pattie Hopson. The couples had been to Marriage Encounter together. Dan and Kathie's daughter was born the same year as Christina. Kathie couldn't help but compare the two girls, realizing that something was wrong. Dan and Kathie had been leading a sharing group of married couples; and when another couple dropped out, they invited the Fosters to join. "Our only mission is to improve our marriages," Kathie explained the first night Ralph and Suzie visited.

The encounter group, which consisted of six couples, met every other week in a different member's home. The first rule was acceptance. The second rule allowed anyone who wanted to respond to a question to say as much as he or she wanted with no one's commenting or criticizing what was said by the responder. "It's unconditional love with no strings attached," Dan said, and Suzie nodded. At each meeting, individuals talked about their personal and marital journeys since the group last met. Suzie and Ralph found it easier to share as time went on especially when no one jumped in with unwanted advice or delivered a judgment that implied they were not doing a good job.

The group's main focus and one of its biggest challenges was accepting as okay whatever each person said or felt. No one offered value judgments. Sharing just is; it's a belief in a journey to God. "If you are on a journey, I want to know about you. That knowledge creates a freedom to love and to care about one another," Dan explained. "One of the main precepts and the heart of the encounter group is dialogue. If you share your feelings with your spouse and then choose to stand in that feeling together, there is a magic. God cared enough about us to limit God's self and to stand with us—we are willing to stand with one another."

That assurance was the greatest gift Suzie, Ralph, and all the others in the encounter group could give one another. They allowed persons to express fully where they were on their journey. The group members allowed Suzie and Ralph to talk about the pain, the anger, and the negativism they felt, because that was where they were on their journey. Instead of comparing or judging, the others simply listened; and in time, they began to understand.

THE FAMILY AND FRIENDS CELEBRATED NATALIE'S BIRTH with the usual baby showers with tiny booties, sun bonnets, and sun dresses. Suzie and Ralph gratefully recorded all of Natalie's firsts in her creamy white baby book with the clean crisp pages. Each trip to the doctor for checkups confirmed that she was a healthy baby girl. "She has crying spells that last a few hours at a time," Suzie told the pediatrician at Natalie's nine-month checkup.

The doctor handed Natalie back to Suzie. "She's a beautiful, healthy, normal nine month old," he reassured her.

Suzie put her apprehension in the back of her mind. Natalie was talking, pulling up and busy learning about her world, just like all of her friends' babies. The doctor's reassurance made Natalie's crying jags seem like a normal occurrence.

With Natalie's birth and the hazy category of undiagnosed with autistic-like traits that specialists assigned to Christina, Suzie and Ralph were exhausted from caring for the two little girls. By the time Natalie was nine months old, Christina was three and a half. She never seemed to sleep. She'd close her eyes for a few minutes, then remain awake for the entire night. She would go on a wild running spree through the house. Sometimes she cried for hours or screamed as if in horrible pain. Ralph and Suzie took turns walking her or rocking her, trying to soothe her endless screaming as they became increasingly exhausted and frustrated. Nothing worked. They had en-rolled Christina at a local school for a time, but Christina did not respond to the behavior modification used by the teachers.

Eventually the Fosters withdrew Christina from the school. Suzie's folks continued to help care for Nikki and Natalie, developing a close relationship and a support system while the search to name what was wrong with Christina continued.

"I DON'T KNOW IF THIS IS GOING TO HELP, but I just watched a film about a boy who is something like Christina," reported the friend with whom Ralph had moved to California. Now beginning seminary, his class had viewed a movie about a boy with a behavior disorder that caused him to withdraw from society into his own private world. The boy seemed very much like Christina and had been labeled autistic. The film showed the method his parents had developed to bring him out of his autism. An institute taught that method.

The news elated Suzie and Ralph. The next day Suzie rushed to the bookstore to purchase a copy of the family's story. "This is our miracle," she exclaimed, a look of joy and relief spreading across her face. With the strong support of the church and the marriage encounter group, Ralph and Suzie decided to learn how to do the program. They learned that the price for the one-week training was $10,000. It was more than they could afford.

Realizing the cost of the young couple's frequent trips in search of a diagnosis for Christina, concerned individuals came up with funding. A check came from Ralph's coworkers. Ralph's parents, Ralph and Gloria Foster, helped with the finances along with Suzie's folks, Darrell and Jeanne Hinkle, who also offered to keep Natalie and Nikki while they learned this new method. It was a heady time of happiness and hope as the whole community embraced the family in their tragedy and future triumph.

It wasn't that Ralph and Suzie didn't adore Christina; they did. But they could not imagine what her life would be like if she continued to deteriorate. They were in a constant state of grief for the child they were losing and for themselves, for what they would miss in a relationship with their child and what they would miss from each other due to the sheer number of hours Christina's care required.

At the institute, they learned the same methods the couple had used on their autistic son. The Fosters learned how to make their home safe, how to join Christina in her own little world, and how to set up a volunteer program. For a solid week, Ralph and Suzie did whatever Christina did—hand slapping, rocking, crawling on their hands and knees, waving ribbons, and twisting their hands.

When they returned home, Suzie was excited and filled with an inner peace. Perhaps at last they had the tools to reach within their child and pull her back from wherever she had retreated.

SOON AFTER THE FOSTERS' RETURN, PATTIE ANNOUNCED at home, "There's a notice on the church bulletin board. Ralph and Suzie are starting a program to help Christina, and they're looking for volunteers."

Mike asked, "What's going on?"

Pattie explained the concept: "They want to have volunteers from morning until night doing whatever Christina is doing."

Pattie shared the information about the training with Kathie Neff who in turn called Suzie. "I'd be interested in helping." Kathie believed that love is a healing force and that the greatest compliment and honor is to meet an individual where he or she is. She began going once each week to meet Christina where she was.

"We can cure her," Suzie had told Kathie and Dan when they returned home. Dan and Kathie were take-charge kind of people, and they spread the word about the need for volunteers.

"These four people are changing our lives," Suzie told Ralph, and she realized that she felt energized for the first time in years. It felt wonderful for someone else to take charge. Suzie and Ralph were independent and strong. They were not the kind of people to ask for help. To ask for themselves would have been impossible, but for Christina they asked.

And so, with the help of their small group, they began the program. Suzie's dad, retired from the construction business, came over and installed an observation window in the bedroom Christina would stay in most of the next two years. Her room was turned into a controlled environment. The bed went into a closet; the shutters were closed to prevent excessive outside stimulation. Suzie added bean bag chairs, while removing clutter, dolls, and toys to reduce visual stimulation. Suzie trained volunteers and recorded Christina's progress through the two-way window. But as the months flew by, only eight volunteers signed up, and the method called for eighty hours of interaction a week. Suzie and Ralph's hope began to fade.

Then, two local newspapers carried Christina's story with an accompanying photograph. The article told the story of Christina's normal birth and development for the first year of her life, followed by the unexplained loss of all her skills and a diagnosis of "undiagnosable" with autistic traits. It described hoped-for goals as a result of the program. It listed the clearly stated goal of two hours per week per volunteer, specified the tasks, and gave a telephone number. Suzie was besieged with calls. The article generated twenty-six new volunteers.

Kathie Neff developed a flyer about Christina's program and organized people to speak about it. The film describing the child who was brought out of autism by his parents, was shown at three Masses at Our Lady of Perpetual Help Church. After the Masses, more than thirty names filled the sign-up sheets—persons who would create large stuffed animals for Christina, interact in her program with her, or pray for her. Suzie had no idea how willing people were to help until the publicity made others aware of an opportunity.

SANDY PODZIMEK was so moved by the movie she had seen on television eight years earlier about the autistic boy, that she immediately recalled it when she saw the flyer on the church door at Our Lady of Perpetual Help. The mother of five children, the idea of helping Suzie with her child appealed to her, and she called to volunteer.

"I'm not working outside the home, so I could give you three mornings a week," Sandy explained. Sandy played games, held Christina's hands, flipped ribbons—always working to make eye contact. The use of music therapy or water therapy often calmed Christina. Or Sandy would gently massage the little girl's legs, reminding her, "I love you."

Working with Christina gave Sandy new insights into both the Foster family and her own family. She had always looked at Suzie and thought, *how beautiful she is; how strong and confident she is.* Over the months, Sandy became aware that Suzie was also someone who was dealing with a lot of pain. When Sandy's session with Christina ended, and a new volunteer arrived, it gave the two women a chance to talk. Suzie could accept the fact that Christina was not normal, but she was grieving for her and for her life. Suzie felt that others did not want her to be depressed, but Christina was her child, and Suzie needed people to accept her grief and mourning. Sandy didn't always know what to say, but she could listen.

For Sandy, working with Christina gave her an opportunity to express love, and it ingrained an attitude of acceptance and letting go. One of her own children had problems with hyperactivity. Through Christina's program, Sandy came to understand that it was something over which the child had no control. An unexpected bonus from helping Christina was discovering new ways to help her own child. Sandy hadn't realized that in reaching out, each person became both the giver and the receiver.

As Pattie Hopson worked with Christina, her children noticed that Christina was a big girl, but she didn't talk. They accepted Christina as a person with feelings who needed their love and care. "You don't need the right words," Pattie explained to them. "You can just give her a smile or a hug."

Pattie remained faithful to Christina's program, coming three mornings a week. And she told other people, "This is okay; this is fun. Suzie is a neat gal." She made a point of encouraging people, telling them that helping was a good experience and that the Fosters really were in need.

As the volunteers continued in their giving, the group of individuals became a community. Pattie's husband, Mike, came straight from work three nights a week to feed Christina. He'd had a poor perception of the amount of time it took to care for Christina while trying to care for a toddler like Natalie. "It's a lot harder than it looks," Mike told Pattie one night. "But until you're right in the middle of it, you don't realize how hard it is."

"Or how much you get out of it," Pattie added.

Mike shook his head in agreement. He had benefited from the program. Mealtime wasn't just shoveling food in. It was a time of trying to coax Christina to have eye contact with him, to get some kind of response from her, as well as trying to keep food out of her lap and hair. "It absolutely thrills me when Christina looks at me with her beautiful eyes," he said.

GROUP MEMBERS CAME TO UNDERSTAND that kids with disabilities need intervention, stimulation, and teaching, which required a difficult balance, not overprogramming. The closed environment allowed Christina to calm down.

Suzie, a marvelous homemaker, loved people. Through Christina's program, once again people were coming into her home. She could do something constructive. Each Sunday night as volunteers met, Suzie and Ralph had a huge meeting with refreshments and reported on Christina's results for the week. Volunteers shared in her small gains.

The caring extended beyond Christina and her family to the larger community. If someone were sick or in the hospital, whoever heard of the illness or need was responsible for organizing meals and letting others know of the need. In this way, Suzie, who spent most of her time at home, could be involved in the calling or food preparation. So it was, that the group members anxiously awaited the call that its newest member had arrived. Pattie and Mike were expecting a baby any moment.

Suzie got the call at 2 A.M. "It's a boy," Mike announced, and there was no mistaking the pride and excitement in his voice.

"What's his name?" Suzie asked, suddenly wide awake.

"Jonathan."

"Is everything okay?"

"Yes. Well, he has a little hole in the top of his mouth, but it can be fixed," Mike said calmly. "Come and visit tomorrow."

"He is so beautiful; he is whole in every other way," Mike and Pattie reassured their friends who stopped by the hospital to welcome the new baby. Because of their experience with Ralph and Suzie, Jonathan's cleft palate was not too shocking for them. True, they did get unwanted pity from some people, but Pattie told them adamantly, "This is something that can be fixed. He can live a normal life."

The mutual caring for one another produced strong friendships within the group. Mike found that he enjoyed spending time with Ralph, who would make time for him emotionally . . . time to talk or time to work on a project that employed Ralph's electrical skills.

After almost a year of Christina's program, Natalie was twenty-two months old. The program, with more than fifty volunteers, was going full swing from 8 A.M. until 10 P.M. each night. It was, Suzie thought, the most wonderful time of her life, exhausting and exciting. Clearly Christina has better eye contact, a longer attention span, and has become calmer.

Suzie was so busy training new volunteers and observing and charting Christina's progress that she didn't dwell on Natalie's subtle changes. She squelched the little pricks of fear that poked at the edge of her consciousness. She knew that if anything happened to Natalie, who was so carefree that they had begun to call her Miss Congeniality, she would lose her mind.

THE HOUSE WAS IMMACULATE. All the guests knew where to put the cold salads, the soft drinks; where to find the potato chip baskets and ice chests. "Come here, Christina," coaxed Mike as Ralph gently handed her into the pool. The Foster family had spent so many warm afternoons in their backyard, surrounded by volunteers and encounter group members who had become friends. They waved ribbons with the girls, holding one of them in the hot tub while deep in conversation about some topic of interest or quizzing Nikki, now thirteen, on her activities.

Suzie stood at the sliding glass door to the patio. She had struggled to allow these people to care for Christina. It reversed what society taught—that you take care of your own—and yet, through Christina and her program, a group of virtual strangers had become family to one another.

"Come on, Natalie, let's go outside," she said, adjusting the strap on her daughter's tiny red and yellow swimsuit. All around the pool, her friends were talking about work and new recipes and trips to the beach and plans for summer vacation. She noticed how the sun glinting on Natalie's dark brown hair gave it a reddish tint. Lazily, she looked across the pool where Ralph, deep in conversation looked relaxed for once, almost happy. He must have sensed her watching him, because he stopped talking abruptly and returned her look.

If Suzie had not had her arms snugly around Natalie, she would have dropped her, so suddenly did Natalie's little body throw itself backward and stiffen, like a child who throws itself to the floor in a wild tantrum. She gripped her tighter, both to keep her from falling and to contain the terror that struck.

Strong arms encircled them, but it was too painful to look up and see Ralph. For in that instant, they both knew that it would be a repeat performance. Whatever Christina had, they knew Natalie had it too.

Within days of Natalie's seizure, the woman who developed Christina's program called. Suzie tearfully related the seizure and Natalie's developmental delays.

"Have you ever heard about a syndrome called Rett syndrome?" the woman asked. "There's a family from Houston whose daughter was diagnosed with autism, but she is now diagnosed with Rett, an extremely rare syndrome. I'm sure they wouldn't mind if you called them," she said, giving Suzie a telephone number.

Suzie immediately called the family and learned the name of Dr. Percy who had diagnosed their little girl. Then she called Dr. Percy and made arrangements to bring the girls to Houston. She had to know.

RALPH AND SUZIE WERE HEARTBROKEN when they arrived at their encounter group. Their balloon of high hopes had burst. If the girls had Rett syndrome, they would not get better. Literature they'd received on Rett was explicit, and it seemed to fit. The diagnostic criteria required for the recognition of Rett syndrome, which occurred exclusively in females with only about 1500 cases diagnosed worldwide, included the following:

A period of normal development until between six to eighteen months. Then began early loss of acquired behavior, social and psychomotor skills. Cognitive functioning in the severely to profoundly retarded range. Loss of acquired purposeful hand skills beginning at age one to four years. Repetitive hand movements including hand washing, hand wringing, hand clapping, and hand mouthing could become almost constant while awake. Shakiness of the torso, which may also involve the limbs, particularly when the child is upset or agitated. Unsteady, wide-based, stiff-legged gait, and sometimes toe-walking.

. . . .

The supportive criteria (symptoms not required for the diagnosis but which may also be seen) included breathing dysfunctions, which include breath holding, or apnea; hyperventilation and air swallowing, which may result in abdominal swelling. EEG abnormalities that include slowing of normal electrical patterns, the appearance of epileptiform patterns, and a reduction in REM (or dream) sleep. Seizures (in up to 80% of patients). Muscle rigidity/spasticity/joint contractures. Scoliosis (curvature of the spine). Teeth grinding. Small feet. Growth retardation. Decreased body fat and muscle mass. Abnormal sleep patterns and irritability. Poor circulation of the lower extremities with the feet and the legs often cold and bluish-red. Decreased mobility with age. Note: All girls do not display all of these symptoms.

That night, Suzie and Ralph poured out their despair. Several nights later at a New Year's Eve party at the Neffs they began to talk again about Natalie. All of their friends were there; and as they looked ahead, the future seemed so bleak that they couldn't help but cry. "Natalie is regressing," they shared. "We don't know if we should put her in nursery school and expose her to normal kids to see if maybe she is just copying Christina, or if she really does have a problem." The group talked late into the night about Natalie.

Two days later, Dan Neff called and said, "We want to get together with you guys. We want to talk to you without the kids." Dan mentioned the name of a local restaurant, and Suzie quickly telephoned her mother and asked her to come stay with the girls.

When everyone was seated and had ordered, Kathie said, "Dan has been beside himself trying to figure out what we can do. He came up with the idea that we could bring Natalie to our house for a few weeks so she can be with normal kids. Then we can tell if she is only copying Christina." Suzie was overwhelmed with the love she felt for them.

"When it comes right down to it, it's not the things of this world that are going to help Natalie or that have helped all of us through the worst of times," Ralph said as they drove home. "It's relationships."

Dan felt that way too. He had joined the Catholic church at about the same time he met the Fosters. Before that he had been a hardcore atheist. Marriage Encounter and experiencing unconditional love had changed his views. He had bought into the church's teaching that everyone was all one family.

"Let's go for it, Dan," Ralph said, when he called the Neffs the next day. The Fosters packed up Natalie's clothing and diapers, and she went to spend a few weeks with the Neffs.

Dan and Kathie got a whole new look at the Fosters lifestyle. At nearly two years of age, Natalie still could not sit alone in a high chair and needed to be spoon-fed, which took a half hour four times a day. "I don't know how you do it," Dan told Ralph at the end of the first week. He knew that when Ralph got home from work, he immediately sat down and rocked Christina to get her settled, sometimes rocking her for hours.

"By the way, the kids adore Natalie," Dan added. "They are practically fighting over her." In turn, the Neffs listened as Ralph and Suzie began to talk more about the fun times they were having with Nikki and how much Christina seemed to be noticing the extra attention she was getting.

Kathie and Dan's offer to keep Natalie was a gift to everyone. The Neffs felt affirmed by offering the Fosters the gift of time with Christina, especially when Natalie was having a good experience with their family.

"We've been busy with little children for a long time," Kathie told her husband late one evening when all the kids were in bed. "But there is no language or interaction between us and Natalie. To experience that for a length of time—longer than the few hours a week we've been spending with Christina—is overwhelming. Think what it must be like. Feeding and care takes so long. All the times Suzie has talked about the messes everywhere, I couldn't relate and understand until now." For Kathie, the experience with Natalie was one she could honestly translate to others. She found herself talking about the Fosters' situation more often.

When the two weeks concluded, the couples got together again to talk about Natalie. Suzie and Ralph sensed how hard it was for Dan to say yes, he thought Natalie had a problem. Natalie's behavior had not changed, but the entire Neff family had.

As they packed up Natalie's clothing and put her car seat back in their station wagon, Suzie waved to Kathie and Dan as Ralph backed out of their driveway. "I feel at peace that we have done all we could do for our girls. They have had the happiest life filled with loving people," she said softly.

THE TIME WAS FAST APPROACHING FOR RALPH AND SUZIE and the two little girls to fly to Houston to meet with Dr. Percy. The hospital personnel would test the girls to see if Rett syndrome was a possibility. After reading the literature, Suzie knew that their children had it, but she wanted it confirmed.

A few weeks prior to their departure, Suzie told Pattie, "I know we're going to be in the hospital setting for a week and that it's going to be a traumatic experience. I've seen these Spinoza bears in a magazine. They are big teddy bears with a wonderful male voice that would be so nice for the girls to take with them, but they cost $300 each."

Just before Ralph and Suzie left, two Spinoza bears showed up.

"How?" Suzie cried, hugging everyone.

Pattie smiled. She had given everyone an opportunity to help purchase the bears. Once again, Suzie realized how many people loved and cared for her family and were supplying their needs. The bears were a testimony to the solid support of a caring community.

The Fosters arrived in Houston when Natalie was two and a half and Christina was five and a half. Cliff and Judy Fry, whose daughter was one of the earliest diagnosed children in this country with Rett syndrome, met them at the airport. The two families bonded instantly. Here, at last, was someone who could understand their search for the name of a rare disorder.

Mark Flapan, Ph.D., a psychologist specializing in the emotional effects of chronic illness on both the individual and the family writes in a NORD (National Organization of Rare Disorders) newsletter:

> Knowledge about your illness, and how it's affecting you, lessens your feeling of helplessness and enables you to feel more in control over what might happen. Although greater knowledge may not, in fact, give you this control, it relieves some of the apprehension related to the unknown. You would rather come to terms with the worst, whatever it might be, than live in the dark—not knowing what might happen. So even if you're upset, frightened or depressed by what you learn, there are many reasons you want to know everything you can about your disease.

Judy and Suzie were convinced Christina had Rett syndrome after comparing the two girls. But at the end of a week of EEGs and sleep studies, the doctors'consensus of opinion was that it was slightly possible. But the doctors could not believe two sisters could have Rett. Dr. Percy referred their case to a colleague in San Diego, California, and the Fosters went home.

SUZIE AND RALPH INCORPORATED NATALIE into Christina's program although they knew Christina was not autistic and that whatever Christina had, Natalie had also.

In retrospect, Suzie thought, *Perhaps it is good that we didn't get a diagnosis then or when Christina was very little and drop the program. The loving support of those in the program is saving my sanity.* The regular arrival of volunteers who had become friends; who cared deeply for her children, no matter what their behaviors were; who pitched in and did some of the physical caring automatically, both saved her physical energy and gave her courage to face another day, knowing she was not alone.

Natalie began to exhibit all the symptoms of Rett syndrome. Her slender frame became distorted with a huge stomach from swallowing air. She hyperventilated, was constipated, and constantly folded one hand into the other or jammed them into her mouth most of her waking hours.

A year and a half after Houston, the Fosters did go to the doctor in San Diego. He diagnosed Natalie with Rett but not Christina. "I can't believe two sisters have the same syndrome," he said. But Suzie and Ralph knew; they were too similar.

At that time, both girls were having seizures. Christina's were so violent and agonizing that her pain was nearly more than Ralph and Suzie could bear. Seizure medication did not control them; and after much soul searching, they agreed that if Christina had a seizure and went into cardiac arrest, they would not intervene.

At an encounter group soon after they made the decision, Suzie shared her awareness of the impending death of her children. Literature about the few diagnosed cases seemed to indicate that girls with Rett syndrome died young, although more recent information indicates that some individuals live into their sixties. Dr. Andreas Rett described the syndrome in 1965, but it was not until 1985 that the Austrian physician examined forty-two girls in the United States. These potential Rett syndrome cases increased the awareness of the syndrome here.

Later Suzie said to Kathie, "I would really like it if you would plan the Mass for Christina's funeral." Suzie's request touched Kathie, and she quickly agreed. Suzie and Ralph's ability to look at death reminded Kathie of the imminence of death and the importance of doing or saying each day what she wanted to say to her family. By facing her own death, Kathie added to her quality of life by making certain she had no regrets about things left undone or unsaid.

LIFE KEPT MARCHING ON AROUND THEM. Nikki was nearing her sixteenth birthday and would soon be driving. Christina was nine and Natalie six. Suzie and Ralph had endured eight years of not knowing for certain that both girls had Rett syndrome. Suzie and Ralph took the girls to Dr. Philipart in Los Angeles. "I want someone to tell me for sure," she told him.

Dr. Philipart took one look and said, "There's no doubt. They both have Rett."

It didn't matter; nothing could help them. They later learned that five cases of sisters with Rett had been diagnosed worldwide. One girl with Rett had been raped and had given birth to a baby with Rett.

Life with two profoundly disabled children, both growing larger and more disabled daily, grew increasingly confining. Suzie struggled to physically carry two girls up and down the stairs. It was impossible to push two wheelchairs. Part of Suzie loved being a mother and homemaker and wanted to be at home with the children. But the other part of Suzie was not fine. She couldn't run errands, couldn't be involved with Nikki. All the major events in Nikki's life were passing by, and usually only she or Ralph went while the other one stayed home. Suzie and Ralph had no time to simply be a couple.

"They have no qualms about what they put into their mouths. You can't keep in the poop—one is eating it. They get it on the carpet; it's on the wall. You can't hold onto both of them—you change one diaper, try to clean up the other child." Suzie and Ralph gave them four baths a day and snacks all the time. "They hyperventilate so they are thirsty all of the time. It's hard to get them to sleep. One is awake, one is sleeping. It's hard to know what they want or what they need."

SUZIE'S PARENTS LOOKED FOR WAYS TO HELP. The diaper service for the girls was about $200 a month. They offered to pay half each month. Suzie's dad provided emotional strength, stopping by to visit and encouraging Suzie's mom to help with the girls. But along with the extraordinary expenses like the girls' nonmotorized wheelchairs, came the pain of minimizing that comes from other people. "You have a husband who makes good money," someone told Suzie.

Suzie realized, *I need my own pain and situation acknowledged—just acknowledge my feelings. No matter how many things I have to be thankful for: a nice home, a caring husband, one daughter who is incredibly lovely and intelligent—there is no happy ending for our two girls and Ralph and me. There will always be an ache. When I go to a high school graduation or a wedding, I'll always think,* that should have happened to Natalie. *But as painful as those thoughts are, what is worse is being systematically dropped from guest lists because someone else feels that it will be painful for us. Joy and pain can be mixed, and we need to feel included, part of the community. We need to choose what we will and won't feel comfortable doing. And, just as other people have milestones, my children do too. Don't act as if my children don't exist. Acknowledge them at Christmas or Easter and on their birthdays. I resent it when they are not acknowledged.*

THE FIRST NIGHT SUZIE AND RALPH ARRIVED at an annual Rett syndrome conference with their Houston friends, Cliff and Judy, they were in a room with 200 parents of Rett girls who knew how they felt.

"This is incredible," Suzie said, as she and Ralph shared concerns and insights with the other couples.

As a woman, Suzie felt that she had an easier time sharing her feelings. Even with Ralph's involvement with a men's group at church, he had never bonded with someone until that conference. There was no feeling like it. The three-day conference offered medical, family, and sibling support. Presentations and panel discussions gave them current information on managing Rett, plus an overview of research into the syndrome. They formed a bond with five or six other couples. They understood the anger a parent with a disabled child can feel toward God. They also asked, "Where is God when we need God?" They too had heard others thanking God for healthy children and wanted to lash out, "What does that mean? God is up there, and God gave me two unhealthy children?"

They too knew the stress of not having the choice of changing jobs because of job-related health care policies and of stunted careers because of the need to stay near support networks. The people they met that night were, for the most part, middle class. They too never qualified for financial help. They too knew that the way to survive was with no dinners out, no movies out.

These parents knew what it was like to split up on the weekends, with one parent at home, while the other parent shopped or went to the movies or out to eat with the other child, just as Suzie did with Nikki. They knew the pain of others' assuming that everything was fine because they saw the two of them out—that it was easy to trade out, that somehow separation of the family was not unnatural.

And the group members had struggled with the numerous manifestations of Rett: "Do they have a headache? Their bones break so easily, but you don't know it until it swells. You may not know until two days later. These children are often fussy. Things bother them, and you can't tell with a thermometer. When a child cries, as a parent you want to fix it, but you don't know what's wrong. How can you tell if it's a toothache, an earache? They all knew only too well that with Rett, from the moment your feet hit the floor in the morning until you go to bed at night, you are dealing with that child. Your dreams die. Your hopes for a normal life die.

Along with the validation the conference gave to Suzie and Ralph, came new insights to siblings' ways of thinking about their family situations. When conference sponsors invited Nikki, an articulate teenager, to be part of a Sibling Panel at a subsequent IRSA (International Rett syndrome Association) conference, she accepted. The message to parents came through loud and clear: Make sure you include your non-Rett kids in the family. Do things out of the ordinary or special for them. Your Rett girls have special needs but so do all children. They need fulfilling and enjoyable activities.

Nikki, as a panel member, shared some of her personal recollections and feelings about having siblings with Rett:

Having sisters with Rett makes you compassionate. Having sisters with Rett is emotionally rewarding—they can love, hate, and respond too. Each is part of the family like anyone else. But the physical requirements can be overwhelming. It can cause you to slow down and look at one another, appreciate one another, and come to grips with who you are to one another as a family.

An audible sigh fluttered across the room, broken by applause. Nikki had used the opportunity to grow instead of becoming angry and turning it inward. She was emerging from her experience healthy. How much of that health came from the space created by volunteers is unknown, but they certainly created some margins that would not have been there.

THE NEIGHBORHOOD SUZIE AND RALPH HAD FIRST SETTLED IN with Nikki had changed. At that time, all the neighbors had been young couples with children. Suzie had watched everyone else's child grow up except hers. When she could stand it no longer she told Ralph, "I've got to get out. I want to move."

Nikki, an active teenager, told them, "I feel like home is not home. I hate it. Everyone wants to visit after working with the girls. We never have a second to ourselves."

Suzie nodded. Nikki was fifteen and received very little of their time. The program, begun three years earlier was losing volunteers as people burned out. Some volunteers brought a friend who waited patiently on the couch. Suzie and Ralph felt they must include the visitor in dinner and conversation, thus their time alone evaporated. Other volunteers wanted to visit or enjoyed the Sunday night's review of the girls' behaviors so much that they stayed late, enjoying the camaraderie. How could they tell all these wonderful people, who were doing this wonderful thing for the girls, to just come, do the program, and leave? While Ralph and Suzie were convinced the program had been exactly what the girls, and the entire family needed, it was time to discontinue the program to gain increased family time.

When people feel trapped and hopeless, changing the situation can help keep them going. In a positive way, the distraction of planning a new home, plus the opportunity for new beginnings can give the family a sense of movement in their own lives.

The Fosters' move to a new home in Corona, California, some twenty minutes away finalized the end. The house and the plans for decorating the interior forced the Fosters to shift gears, focusing their energies and talents on creating something unique.

Suzie sensed negative feelings from a few of their volunteers: *How dare they stop the program, move to a big new home, and abandon the old community?* Others were supportive, realizing that Suzie and Ralph were doing what they felt was best for their whole family.

THE DESIGN OF THE NEW HOUSE centered around the girls' needs. Christina and Natalie had their own gated wing of the house with music, television, soft toys, bean bag chairs, and waterbeds.

Natalie, more hyperactive than Christina, has two gears: asleep or on the move. She is happy and congenial and has many classic Rett symptoms—hand movements, hyperventilation, spasticity, and loss of cognitive skills.

Christina is affected more physically than Natalie and has a severe seizure disorder. Christina doesn't feel good; she's frail, thin, and cries a lot. The seizures or the disorder seem to cause a lot of pain, and she screams all night. As Suzie watches Ralph gently rocking Christina in the rocking chair they'd bought with such high hopes, she thinks, *Even now—after all of these years, Ralph is the most wonderful father. He rocks or walks the floor all night long with one of the kids, then gets up and goes to work.*

MARY O'CONNELL walked up the neatly trimmed sidewalk and gazed at the Fosters' two-story house before her—the outside a rich cream-colored stucco. Spying the white ceramic ducks that peeked out from the lush ivy planted alongside the garage, she smiled to herself. *How like Suzie.* Although she had known Suzie and Ralph for six years, she had not been involved with the Fosters in the early years because she had her own anxiety that kept her separate. Mary and her husband, Mike, had been a part of the encounter sharing group and had recently renewed their relationship with the Fosters.

"I'm so glad you came," Suzie said, welcoming Mary inside.

"Me too." The house looked like a miniature doll shop. Family pictures of Suzie or Ralph or Nikki—always holding Christina and Natalie, dotted the walls. *She's a lot like me,* thought Mary. *She presents a perfect exterior; she doesn't show what's inside.*

The issue of loss was something the two women shared. The more a person invests himself or herself in the care of a disabled child, the more at risk a parent can become in his or her ability to set boundaries or differentiate their own needs from those of the child.

"Let's sit in here with our coffee," Suzie suggested, leading Mary to the den. Mary settled into the couch and pulled a well read book from her purse.

"Thank you, Suzie. This book has been a great healing for me," Mary said, laying *Before and after Zachariah* on the coffee table. The book related the story of what life is like in the home of a child who is severely brain-damaged and whose parents eventually placed him in a residential care facility.

Suzie nodded. She'd given the book, which also described the impact a profoundly disabled child has on a marriage, to several of her friends and waited to see what people would do with it. Books, movies, and groups provide avenues for opening up emotions and dealing with them.

Mary shared the emotions that different parts of the book had unleashed. As Suzie began to open up emotionally, Mary realized that the book had created a place where both of them could meet. They shared their grief. Their losses were equal but different; pain was pain. At the close of their visit, they felt connected. Each had tried to communicate tentatively with others so many times but had not found that safe someone who understood the sense of emptiness that is never quite filled. A strong friendship was developing out of their separate tragedies.

Mary knew that she had a gift for Suzie, a gift that another friend had given her—the gift of support no matter what. During her time of pain, a supportive person called Mary daily. Even when that person felt that the outcome would be bad, the friend took the risk. If Mary wanted to talk, they'd talk; otherwise the friend said, "I'll call you tomorrow," and she did.

"Suzie, I felt so disconnected from the world that I couldn't function. I became so depressed that I tried to will myself to die. You can't will death; so you go on, dead inside. You don't even know why you go on. But you wake up, and in order to survive in our society you have to smile, get dressed, present yourself well. Tragedy doesn't make people feel well. If you can't express it, your personality dies, your body dies . . . just enough. Go ahead and tell people you are hurting. If you need to scream, scream. Personally, I like to break dishes. If you need to fall apart and not get up and clean, do it. Stop letting people see it as simple and easy. Quit protecting everyone from your struggle and reveal the consequences. If you manage it well, most people think there's no problem. Most people want to make those situations invisible. If you can keep the problem neat and clean or upstairs, it's okay. The problem is not the handicap, it's the estrangement of the heart—you can't identify with others."

"People ask me why I get so upset. They tell me I have so much," Suzie said. "Ralph and I have talked about this so many times. We'd give it all away, if not having money would make it different."

Mary provided a nonjudgmental ear that came from realizing that arguments, tears, anger, and depression could be the result of a stressful time with the girls. "Okay, so there's tension," she'd say. "So let's have coffee and not let the tension interfere with the purpose of a visit, which is to give and get support."

Mary encouraged visits from Suzie and the girls, which gave Suzie a change of scenery free from worry about the girls' behavior. "When the girls are at my house, it doesn't matter if they break something. I can clean, and I can buy something new—things just aren't important." Her body language reinforced what she was saying.

Mary also saw that Ralph and Suzie needed others to keep an eye on the girls as they wandered from room to room; people who, instead of sitting and watching them, got up and tended to Christina or Natalie. Only then could the parents get a break. Because the girls had no stamina and extremely poor coordination, they used wheelchairs for mobility. Often Mary and Suzie would stroll the girls in their wheelchairs around and around the backyard. Mary knew that she must enter Suzie and Ralph's world, if she wanted to have a relationship with them.

MIKE and Ralph were becoming close friends too. In his own life, Mike's friends had come to him during a crisis and said, "We thought you might want someone to talk to. If you want, we're available." Looking back, he realized they risked rejection. He had needed them and poured his heart out to them. Because of his own experience, Mike knew that he didn't have to be superhuman or wise to help a friend. He only needed to listen, to show interest, and to allow the hurting friend to speak.

Mike had never been good at small talk. If someone had said, "Go help Foster and be supportive," he couldn't have done it. That would have been too direct. Being a friend to Ralph evolved out of doing things with him and out of being open and honest. For a long time Mike had wanted to relandscape nearly an acre of his property. Together, the two men planned the fencing; made trips to the hardware store; and agreed that as an electrical engineer, Ralph would plan the lighting. When Ralph needed help, Mike showed up. Mike and Ralph's work time became a time to share feelings.

THE FOSTERS WERE EXPERIENCING MANY LIFE CHANGES. The week before Suzie's fortieth birthday, her father thought he had pneumonia. Three months later, he died of lung cancer. Suddenly, the person Suzie had always known would be there for her was gone.

Suzie's mother now lived twenty miles away instead of a street away. She was getting older and so was Suzie. Suzie found herself alone in a big house with two completely helpless kids. As he became more successful, Ralph's job had become more demanding and he was not as available. The future became frightening to contemplate.

Suzie realized they needed to consider placing the girls in a residential care facility. She did not want Nikki to spend her whole life struggling to care for her sisters. "What would happen to her if she had to figure out what to do with the girls?" she asked Ralph. As a panelist for the Rett syndrome conference, Nikki had voiced her feelings clearly when she told the audience:

I think a question of placing a member of your family in institutional care is very, very difficult. I love my sisters so much that I never want to come home and not have them be there. My mom and dad are the strongest people I know.

I know placing them is so difficult because they are your family. I've grown up with them, and I don't know anything different. I just want them to always be in a good place. If we could find a home where [they] could get that love and devotion, I would feel better about that decision.

The Fosters had looked for a residential care home placement facility for the girls for several years. They finally found one that met their expectations. The owner had met Natalie and Christina and was enthusiastic about having them come. If they decided to place the girls, they would be one and one-half hours away from them.

"I love caring for them," Suzie told Mary one day as she and Ralph wrestled with their decision. "I'm just so tired."

As Suzie and Ralph made plans for placement, Mary saw the ups and downs of not being emotionally and psychologically ready. They thought Natalie and Christina would move to their new home June 1, but California's budget shutdown stopped all funding. Suzie and Ralph had been told that when they received the call saying Natalie and Christina were approved, that they must have them at the facility on the first day of the coming month. Each month they waited and on Thanksgiving Day, 1992, they received the call. They had less than a week to prepare for the move emotionally.

Mary called Suzie daily. No matter how their conversations went, Mary made sure that Suzie and Ralph knew they were available day or night. "It's okay to cry, to feel ugly, to be as angry as you need to be; it won't scare me away," Mary said. As Suzie sobbed, Mary held her. "This is a scary thing—you be whoever you need to be. If you're not pretty or well dressed or you scream or curse, I won't be driven away because the common denominator of our experience is that I did not feel pretty or understood. Most people get to live so they always show their best side, but these circumstances bring out a person inside who frightens you and who you don't know." Mary knew she would serve as the lifeline back to community for Suzie, just as someone else had been for her.

How wonderful to have a friend who doesn't judge, reflected Suzie, wiping her eyes. She could be herself without feeling guilty or ashamed for being out of control. The night before the girls were to move to the group home, Mary's telephone rang.

"We need you to go with us," Suzie said.

"Of course we'll come," Mary agreed.

CHRISTINA AND NATALIE HAD BEEN IN THE GROUP HOME a month. Suzie and Ralph had visited them six times. One Saturday afternoon as Ralph and Suzie drove home from a visit with the girls, he dialed Mike from their car phone. It had become a ritual to check in with one another every Saturday.

"Where are you guys?"

"Coming from visiting the girls."

"Come for dinner," Mike's voice conveyed excitement. Ralph had enriched his life. Ralph was a good role model in terms of understanding the potential of what a good father can be. At the age of forty-six, Mike still had two children at home, and his relationship was deepening with them in a way that he had never believed possible. Ralph had become a good friend to Mike and Mary's children too. They talked about the term *family of choice*, and Ralph and Suzie definitely fit into that category.

Ralph smiled and asked Suzie, "How's dinner sound?"

Suzie responded, "Tell them we'll pick up buns and hamburger meat for the grill." It was good to have a place to go.

While the men went off to survey their fencing, Suzie and Mary talked about the kids. Mary was able to gently remind her friend, "You didn't give your girls away. You put them in an environment so you can have reserves of energy for kissing, loving, and hugging. They belong with you, and you can get them any day you want. And you can change your mind."

Mary and Mike had visited the group home with the Fosters soon after the girls had moved in. They played with the other children there so Ralph and Suzie could devote their time to Natalie and Christina. Mary also made a point of telephoning Suzie. "How's Natalie doing?" Mary asked when Suzie answered the telephone. Suzie had commented the day before that Natalie had had a fever. Sometimes the topic of the girls was only a small part of the conversation, but Mary always acknowledged them.

Suzie and Ralph want the girls to be remembered, to have their special days remembered and celebrated, and to have an opportunity to share information about their girls. Perhaps that is why their friendship with Mike and Mary has deepened. They understand the love the Fosters have for their girls and understand placement as a loving choice.

EACH PERSON WHO TOUCHED CHRISTINA AND NATALIE'S LIFE has been changed forever. Mike, Pattie, and their children, having experienced the love they had for the girls at an unconscious level, moved to a ten-acre ranch for one and one-half years as houseparents to a group of disabled individuals living in Christian community. They found that the universal language is a smile and a hug. Their family had no fear of disability because Christina and Natalie had taught them about the person behind the disability.

Nikki has a respect for the brevity of life and has come to value her own personal strength, a gift from her sisters. She is eager to spread the news of Rett syndrome. Sandy Podzimek has gained an awareness that pain can lie beneath a beautiful, calm exterior—everyone has struggles.

Dan Neff, who experienced unconditional love through Marriage Encounter, has been able to act on the teachings of the Catholic church that we are all one family. Kathie Neff will never look at a family with a disabled family member without realizing how painfully different it is to have a child who never leaves home. Yes, there was a beautiful innocence and reverence—but a realization that it was not always lovely.

Mary and Mike understood the importance of just listening—someone had shared that gift with them, and they passed it on.

EPILOGUE
Suzie writes the following:

> It's been a year since placement. Nikki has graduated from college, and I am working outside the home. Ralph and I have lived through unimaginable grief. We've come through in one piece as a strong couple and strong parents to Christina and Natalie even though they are not living with us in our home on a daily basis.
>
> The girls have adjusted better than I could have ever hoped for. The caregivers at Valley Children's Home have fallen in

love with both girls, and they seem to have captured the hearts of everyone in their new school. When they are home now, they are the stars—we can't get enough of them. In fact we fight over who's going to hold them next.

Natalie and Christina are very happy, well-adjusted little girls. All of our lives have been enriched to some degree. It's not the life we dreamed of fourteen years ago, but it is the best we could do with what we were given.

POSTSCRIPT

In February 1994, the directors at the children's home pronounced Christina too fragile medically to remain. Through the help of a caring caseworker and a consultation with their attorney, Ralph was able to get a Medicaid waiver that funds 120 hours of in-home care weekly for Natalie and Christina. Wanting to keep the girls together, Suzie and Ralph will move both girls home soon—a move their entire family eagerly anticipates. ❖

Linda

IT WAS EASY TO TELL THIS WAS NOT HER PLACE. At 5'8", Linda Harry was much taller and fairer than the people she met in the Middle East. It didn't matter. Her easy, outgoing nature and sincere desire to help others had brought her to Israel to work for a summer on an archaeological dig. Her friend, Jan Gallop, was with her. They learned how to backpack, to set up tents, and to hike long distances before beginning to dig. The hard work didn't matter; Linda loved a challenge.

"You've got the wanderlust." Jan had laughed as they boarded the drab, olive-green truck that had taken them from one end of the Middle East to the other during the past ten weeks. In another week they'd be flying home to Portland, Oregon, where Linda would finish a final semester of graduate school and begin work as a bacteriologist at a local hospital.

"I know. I'll always find a way to work in the mission field," Linda replied. Just out of college and on her fourth short-term missionary trip, Linda'd had lots of adventures. She'd spent three summers in Korea in a national tuberculosis hospital doing rural clinics and laboratory work, even some minor surgery and assisting when a need arose. She had majored in microbiology at California State University in Long Beach and enjoyed using her skills.

"Life will seem dull when we get back home," Jan said, as the truck pulled up at the dig site. Linda smiled and climbed down. It would be another hot, dusty day, but she was used to the heat; she'd grown up in southern California.

"True. This has been an incredible journey. Wait until I tell my sister Suzi about being sold as a Bedouin bride for twelve camels because they liked my long blond hair." She couldn't wait to share lots of other things with her only sibling who was four years older and who worked as an interior designer—things like camping in a Crusader castle, showers in a waterfall in the middle of the desert, and hiking up Mount Sinai to see the sun set and again to see it rise. She hated to leave, but there would always be next year.

THE REFLECTION THAT STARED BACK from the bathroom mirror in her Portland, Oregon apartment would have frightened Linda, but she was just too tired to care. Frankly, she had gotten used to it. Gone were the golden skin tones of the summer; the freckles that had given her a perky, fresh look; the toss of the head that said, "Let me do that!" Down the hall the telephone was ringing.

"Linda." The impatience in her roommate's voice was barely disguised as she held out the telephone and waited for Linda to shuffle down the hallway. Linda knew her roommate thought she was a hypochondriac.

"Hello."

"Don't get excited. I thought you should know that there's been an accident." The strain in Suzi's voice made Linda shudder. "Linda, Dad's broken his neck, and they're going to put him in a cast. He'll be in the hospital at least a month and in a body cast from his neck to below his waist for six months." Quickly Suzi told her sister what she knew: that their father had fallen from a ladder

"I'm worried about Mom," Linda said. "I'm coming home."

Home was Hermosa Beach, a southern California paradise of surf and sand. They were a close family, and it disturbed Linda to see her dad, just getting ready to retire, stuck in a hospital in so much pain. She knew it was hard on her mother too. She decided to keep her own struggles with exhaustion to herself. She'd scheduled an appointment with another new doctor for next week. She had seen six doctors with two hospitalizations but no diagnosis. Hopefully this new doctor could diagnose her.

THE PAIN CAME IN WAVES that made her abdomen feel as if it were on fire. "Not now," Linda moaned, clutching her stomach. She couldn't afford to feel this sick with her father upstairs in the hospital's critical care unit. Could this in some way be related to whatever was making her so dead tired? She'd been tested previously for parasites since she'd lived overseas, but that had turned up negative. Another doctor suggested that Linda see a psychologist. She had; but she knew whatever it was, it was not in her head. The pain that stabbed her now was real enough.

"Linda, I'm taking you to the emergency room," Suzi informed her in her big-sister, no-nonsense voice.

This time Linda was not arguing. Her blue eyes, bloodshot as usual now, were blinking back tears. "Suzi, I'm not crazy. I know something is wrong. I've been thinking it might be a brain tumor, but now with this. . . . I just can't figure it out." Her voice trailed off.

Suzi hurt for her sister. Linda had friends in Portland. Jan was checked in on Linda, and someone else drove her to and from work. But that was no way to live—with someone dragging her up the stairs to her apartment so she could lie in bed, wracked with pain and exhaustion until the next workday .

"It's got to be kidney stones," the emergency room intern said as she and Suzi awaited test results. That would be a relief; doctors could remove kidney stones. But tests revealed no stones.

"LINDA." THE VOICE WAS KIND. She looked up to see her warm family doctor and to hear again the words she had heard so many times. This time though, she was listening. He was the only person in the medical profession who had been determined to find out what was wrong. He did not think it was in her head.

He sat beside Linda in his ever so familiar office—the kind of office she might have. She could help people if she could just get well. "Linda, you've got to quit your job and come home. Listen, there's a medical conference in Denver in a few months. I want you to come. There may be some answers for us there."

It did not seem possible to the twenty-two-year-old Linda that she'd have to move home after all her glorious plans to travel, to go on to medical school. She was down to 115 pounds and unable to concentrate on the smallest tasks because of the pounding pain in her head. She was a tired weakling. "Okay. I'll come to Denver."

"CORN?" SUZI COULD NOT BELIEVE IT. "Yes," the family doctor confirmed, "Linda had an immune reaction to corn. She reacted so strongly to it, she has been in a coma for the past twenty-four hours. She's coming out of it now. I've made an airline reservation for her to fly home tomorrow. Let me give you the flight numbers."

"Then what?" Suzi asked.

"Then we're going to make arrangements to get her into an isolation unit to test her immune system."

This is crazy, Suzi thought, calling work to let them know she'd be taking the next day off. She'd already missed a number of days helping with her father. It wasn't that she minded. She loved taking care of her family, but she needed to keep her job too.

Linda had gone back to Portland to quit her job. She'd also managed to pack up her things and visit with Jan. "I'm going to miss our weekly get-togethers," Jan said.

"Me too."

"I'll come see you," Jan promised.

Then Linda was gone. She went home to Hermosa Beach for two months to await an opening at the Dallas, Texas isolation unit. When the call came, she was ready.

THE SPECIALIST AT THE DALLAS HOSPITAL WAS BRISK, flipping through her paperwork, a thick worn stack attached to a chart. He cleared his throat and sat down in the visitor's chair by her hospital bed. "We've rarely found anyone so reactive. The exposure to the toxic chemicals you work with has caused your immune system to fail. Your immune system can no longer recognize what it should fight. Instead of fighting bacteria and viruses, it now fights foods, chemicals, and your own tissues. That is why you reacted so strongly to corn. The name of your condition is vasculitis secondary to immune defects."

Linda breathed a sigh of relief. "I quit that job."

The doctor shook his head. "Linda, you're going to have to be in a special environment for a long time. Can someone in your family get down here for a consultation so we can make plans?"

Linda had longed for people to come and visit her in the hospital and wondered how other patients survived long stays in far away hospitals, separated from family. The few friends she did have in Dallas stopped by occasionally to see how she was doing. Just knowing for those few minutes that she was not alone made her feel connected and relieved the heavy load of stress that built up.

"Hey kid."

Linda carefully turned her head to look toward the hospital room door. "Suzi!" Forgetting, she tried to sit up, but the pain was too much. Quickly Suzi was at her side. The months of sitting with her father as he recovered from his broken neck had taught her not to wait to give help or to make the patient do the getting up or turning to see her. "Here, let me sit at the end of the bed, so you don't have to twist around so much."

Once seated, Suzi asked, "What's happening down here?" It relieved Linda to pour out the whole painful mess. She wasn't whining, just letting it all out.

The unreality of what was happening to Linda was slowly sinking in. Coming to the hospital in Dallas was not the end of Linda's problems as they'd hoped. It was the beginning of a long journey that her sister could not make alone. On the telephone with Linda's doctors, Suzi began to see that she would need to take care of Linda. The doctor had been blunt. "In five years, Linda will either have made it or be dead. She is what is called a universal reactor. Almost every substance she comes in contact with creates an immune reaction; fumes from a car exhaust to popcorn cooking all trigger a reaction."

Strongly committed, Suzi and her parents agreed they would do whatever it took to bring Linda home and to get her as well as she could be.

FOUR MONTHS AFTER LINDA HAD CHECKED HERSELF into the Dallas isolation unit, she was on her way home, barely conscious after breathing the fumes from airplane fuel. Everything in the airplane— synthetics, perfume, food odors, plastics—triggered a reaction. Suzi, who was traveling with her this time, was frightened and appalled at how quickly Linda collapsed. When they got home, Suzi would begin working to fix an apartment for Linda at their parents' home in Hermosa Beach. Suzi lived in an apartment behind her parents' beach house.

Suzi saw that Linda's need for a safe room was immediate. Frustrated that the hospital had not given her adequate guidelines for preparing the room prior to Linda's release, Suzi and her dad frantically set to work. They stripped all the wallpaper off the walls and removed everything from the room. Because Linda reacted to almost everything, clothing and bedding could be made only of untreated cotton. Her furniture had to be made of metal or certain hardwoods.

The little house was just a block from the beach. Linda, wrapped in a down comforter, and her mom would be down at the beach all night long, while Suzi and her dad put down linoleum and hung foil wall paper, according to hospital directions.

Reacting wasn't the word Suzi would use for what happened to Linda. Just seeing Linda start to fade as her body swelled from the inside, knowing that her brain was swelling too and that eventually she would lapse into a coma, made them hurry with their task. Both Suzi and Bill Harry worked during the day; they had only the evenings to create Linda's room. No one was telling them exactly what to do. They knew they must cover the walls with foil to seal the chemicals behind the walls out. They'd also gotten rid of everything made of petrochemicals, plastics, carpets, detergents, household cleaners, synthetic curtains, pesticides, books, magazines, and natural gas.

That night after they finished the room, Suzi and her dad walked together past the small beach homes that were clustered just a few feet from one another and across the strand to the street next to the beach where cars were not allowed. The spot was an ideal retirement home for her parents. They'd purchased it as a weekend getaway, never dreaming Suzi and Linda would be coming home to stay. The front of the house had two bedrooms. Later they'd added the back apartment and garage. A tiny yard separated the two buildings.

"IT'S READY," SUZI CALLED. "COME ON, YOU'LL LOVE IT."

When the little group finally made it back to the house, Suzi couldn't help but be grateful that she could get her sister inside---safe from all the suntan lotion, perfumes, and odors from foods on the beach. It seemed everything everywhere was dangerous to Linda.

Within minutes Linda cried, "Suzi, something is wrong. I'm feeling very nauseated. Are you certain that is foil paper?"

"Of course. I told the clerk twice it had to be foil."

It was too late to replace the foil that night. Linda had to endure another day until Suzi and Bill could figure out why it wasn't working and replace it.

"Guess I'm not doing too good," Suzi said. "Sorry."

"It's okay," Linda said. "Really."

Linda felt guilty that Suzi and her folks were working so hard to help her, and all she could do was sit.

"Listen, Linda. This is not going to be too bad," Suzi promised that night. She'd discovered that foil creased. What they had put up was wallpaper made of mylar. Both types looked alike, but mylar was made with petrochemicals. "Dad and I really have the hang of this wallpaper stuff. Just go to the beach, stay away from everyone, and we'll be done in a few hours."

Suzi could have kicked herself for the mistake. They had wasted precious hours for nothing. Next time she would be more careful, but for now, all she could do was hang the foil paper while her dad pulled down the mylar. They soon discovered that the right materials were elusive. Linda reacted to the patterned foil. They rehung plain foil. The linoleum made her sick. They replaced it with ceramic tile. Twice they called paramedics when Linda could not stop vomiting and suffered heart pain. Paramedics administered an injection into her heart to calm the fibrillating but were advised by Linda's doctors not to transport her.

Because Linda was unable to withstand a hospital environment, Suzi learned to give her sister IVs with saline and vitamin C to keep her hydrated. Suzi began to believe that if her sister died, it would be her fault for not doing enough.

LINDA'S PAIN WAS RELENTLESS. She couldn't take aspirin. Her joints and her brain swelled, leaving her in agony all of the time. She needed a quiet house with the lights on low; and when she was having reactions, which was virtually all of the time, she needed darkness. They ordered a special cotton mattress from Dallas for her.

"How much was it?" Linda asked, when it arrived.

"Don't worry about it," Suzi said kindly. They had to find other things too. The new plastic bathtubs were made with petrochemicals; Linda needed a metal tub. Since Linda could tolerate no type of heat, they poured nonchlorinated hot water into the tub to help warm the room.

Linda could not shop, cook, or do laundry—let alone work. She needed help to dress and bathe. Initially she lost consciousness almost every day. Within months she had gone from being a self-supporting career woman to being a helpless invalid. She did not tell anyone, but she was becoming suicidal. She felt that her life had no value because everything was done for her. For Linda, doing things equaled value. She wrestled with God for years over that issue. Linda finally came to understand that it's not what I do, but who I am that matters. Each time she and Suzi talked, she felt herself become grounded again.

"What is reasonable?" Suzi demanded, late one afternoon.

"What do you mean?"

"I mean, let's be realistic. Right now you can't work. The chemicals in printer's ink make it impossible for you to read. You can't use a computer because the chemicals in them would kill you. You can't talk on the telephone. So what is reasonable to expect of yourself?"

After talking and thinking about it for a while, they decided that listening to one verse of scripture and praying for ten minutes each day was reasonable at that time.

WHILE THE ENVIRONMENT LINDA'S FAMILY CREATED FOR HER was as safe as they could make it, she alternated time at home with emergency flights back to the Dallas isolation unit for months at a stretch. Each trip to the Dallas hospital whittled away at the Harrys' bank account. Linda had worked for a year, and she had put little away for a medical emergency. Right now the expense of emergency travel, hospitalizations, medications, house renovation, the purchase of non-treated natural fiber clothing and bedding, all added up.

Linda required a special food supply from a mail order company since it had to be chemically free. Much of her food had to be exotic, since she became sensitized to each food that she ate and could not eat the same item again for months or more. A combination of two foods a day was allowed. Quail, mango, buffalo, antelope, pear, papaya, lettuce, yams, lion, filberts, and so on became her diet.

"It seems like I am destroying my family," Linda told her family when her father continued to work past his scheduled retirement.

"Linda, we are in this together," her father gently told her when she apologized for her illness. "It didn't just happen to you; it happened to all of us, and God is using it for all of us."

JAN GALLOP did not forget her friend. It was hard to believe she'd have to read the ingredients to everything she ate to be certain it contained no garlic and use special bath and laundry soaps to prepare for their meeting. She had put away her perfume and hair spray bottles to keep from accidentally giving herself a spray, thus "contaminating" herself before the visit.

Even with all Jan's precautions, the family found that it was better for Linda to visit with outside people on the beach, where the wind could blow any scent away. Jan sat looking out at the water. Hundreds of sea birds fluttered, landed, then lifted off again.

"I used to love to walk in the sand after a storm and see what had washed ashore or been uncovered by the wind," Linda said.

"That doesn't surprise me," Jan said, picking up a shell. "It's a beautiful beach."

Linda sighed; she was a prisoner on the beach. "Yes. But Jan, this is not normal. Life is not like this. This is not a normal life." The pain in Linda's voice was unmistakable.

"Linda, this life you are living now is normal. You have to accept it as normal."

The next day Linda said to Jan, "I needed to hear that this is normal for me now." Jan smiled. She loved to visit Linda because they shared a friendship, and she could bring her the gift of the outside world. Linda wanted to know all about what was going on in Portland. It was hard to see her so isolated, knowing how on the go she used to be.

Jan also was a healthy outsider to whom Linda could vent her feelings. Because Jan had established a relationship with Linda already, she encouraged her to share by saying, "Okay, what is going on?" Simply listening without analyzing, moralizing, or trying to change Linda's mind about the way she was feeling, kept the doors of communication open between the two. When she couldn't visit, Jan wrote letters.

Linda shared family concerns with Jan—her parents' health, Suzi's giving up her life for her, the uncertainty that drained everyone as doctors experimented with treatments or regimens. As they talked, Linda worked through the dynamics of grief, grieving the many losses associated with her illness. "I'm not independent anymore; I don't even look like the same person," Linda said, sadly. All of the things that defined her—appearance, activities, relationships—had changed.

As Linda changed, so did Jan. She told her friend one day, "Because of you, I am now more aware of people and their needs." Knowing Linda, who at times looked fairly well, made Jan sensitive to others who looked well but in fact were not. She was becoming aware of not just Linda but other people with difficult circumstances.

Someone had told Linda, "You'll do better with new people if you say everything is fine." Jan had seen other people with long-term illnesses, and she never knew when Linda would underplay how sick she felt, trying to focus on what she could do rather than how lousy she felt. Often the energy it took to look "normal" wore Linda out faster than she wanted to admit. The result of trying so hard to look well meant that after a visitor left, she was severely ill for hours.

WHILE LINDA AND HER FAMILY BEGAN THE LONG PROCESS of adjustment, others began to surface as possible helpers. "If you need anything, call," different individuals said. Suzi did not know what to expect, but she knew they had to freeze or can all of Linda's food as it came in season to assure that it was grown without the use of growth enhancers, pesticides, or chemical fertilizers. Her mom had never canned, and she was trying to figure out how. Suzi picked up the telephone. She would accept the help of other people.

When the day for canning arrived, Suzi was elated that several of the people who had offered, arrived with canning jars and instructions. "Thank you for coming," she said.

"We're getting more out of helping than you know," they replied. It was fun; helping and visiting made everyone feel good.

As Suzi, tall and fair like her sister, stood barefooted in the kitchen surrounded by dozens of jars filled with safe fruits and vegetables, she breathed a sigh of relief. "There's no way we could have done this alone," she said when they sealed the last jar.

As Linda lay in her protective room, separated by glass and foil from the women who had come to help prepare her food, she thought, *Even when everything else is out of control, God is in control.* She needed people to bond with her by going through the struggle with her family.

As Linda tried to come to terms with her illness, Suzi looked for some balance. The first year, she had come home from work each day with a horrible feeling in the pit of her stomach, wondering, *How will I find her?* No matter how much she tried to control Linda's reactions by proper medication, rest, and food, her sister continued her downward spiral.

Each time the family rushed Linda back to Dallas, the question arose, *Will she come home again?* The isolation unit, which consisted of 125 beds for subacute care and 35 beds for acute care, housed people like Linda. Some had lived there for seventeen years. To the Harry family and the doctors, this strange illness was real, terrifying, and easily fatal. But some members of their community fed them a message that Linda was okay, creating an environment in which the family felt compelled to defend Linda's diagnosis.

No simple solutions existed. Everyone wanted a quick-fix answer, but this time there wasn't one. Linda told Jan, "We are geared in society to eliminate pain, struggle, and frustration. People are irate that I don't get better or worse or die."

Many people simply disappeared from Linda's life. In our fix-it, utilitarian, outcome-oriented society, many persons can't tolerate a long-term illness.

AS LINDA'S FAMILY TRIED TO PROVIDE FOR HER, it was natural to share with others in normal conversation the dramatic turn their lives had taken. Bill and Margaret Harry, Linda and Suzi's parents, had attended Grace Community Church some forty miles distant for several years.

CINDY BUCHAN also attended Grace Community Church, where she learned of Linda's special needs. When the announcement came from the pulpit that persons would participate in writing the Bible in pencil for Linda because Linda was allergic to ink, Cindy thought, *What a great idea. Maybe I'll help.*

GENE NEWMAN was also a member of Grace Church. Gene was involved with ACAMPAR (a Spanish word for camping), a camping program for persons with disabilities. When the church's Bible-writing project had gotten underway, Gene had written out the first nine chapters in the Book of Numbers for Linda. Knowing that he had a part in something that significant and seeing others take that opportunity to be connected and to serve, underscored Gene's feelings that many people are looking for service. He believed that they become spiritually mature through service.

"This is the way I see it working," Gene said to Linda one afternoon. "You are challenged. You accept something a bit beyond you and for whatever reason, you grow into it."

Linda was overwhelmed when church members delivered fifteen notebooks from the Bible writing project. She hadn't read anything since she became ill. The pencil-written manuscript included so many different writing styles. The number of people who had written for her was astounding. One eight-year-old boy's participation had led his parents to visit Linda. When they learned that Linda needed a freezer for her food, they offered the one they were no longer using.

Gene's concern was that someone from his church had a need and was lonely. He had first heard of Linda's illness from Bill Harry at a meeting and was surprised to learn that they lived only a few blocks away from each other. He began to visit in an attempt to brighten her days, bringing WAYNE, a coworker in the ACAMPAR program, with him. Suzi, Wayne, and another friend, GARY, shared a rare sense of humor, delighting in making Cindy and Linda laugh hysterically at their antics. For Linda, it was good to see Suzi relax into the comedian that she had been before Linda had become so sick. As the group talked and sang or dressed up in kimonos and did skits, Linda leaned towards Suzi and whispered, "How do other people make it without friends like these?"

By coming to visit Linda, the group members also became aware of her needs. They'd shivered in identical cotton shirts in the tiny, unheated foil bedroom. When someone suggested they turn on the heat, Suzi reminded them that it was impossible. The next time the group came to visit, they brought a down coat for Linda.

Although Linda lived more than an hour from Cindy, Cindy decided she would continue to visit. She often thought about Linda, whom she considered to be sweet and undemanding. Cindy was dismayed when Linda said, "I hate to say this, but the cologne stays in your hair even though you stop wearing it a week before you come. I can smell it, and it makes me sick. Could you please not wear it any more?"

It wasn't too hard to give up her special shampoo and soap for the unscented kind that didn't make Linda react. But this was asking for something more than Cindy felt ready to give. Frankly, she was a little angry.

On the way home that afternoon, Cindy wrestled with her emotions. *I gave up so much,* she thought. Realizing what it cost Linda to risk their friendship, knowing that Cindy could just as easily walk away, she decided to honor Linda's wishes. It wouldn't be fair to just drop out of Linda's life.

DON and ANNETTE, a retired couple from the church, took Bill Harry up on his invitation to visit. *Where does she get her food if she's allergic to everything?* they wondered aloud. Mr. Harry explained, "We're ordering wild meat from a company back East."

"That must be expensive," said Don. "Those are the types of animals I hunt. I also do a lot of fishing. As long as it just needs to be wild and all natural, the places where I hunt in the mountains are uncontaminated. I'd like to help provide her food." Soon after, Don began to deliver the meats and fish as soon as he got it. He brought it wrapped and ready to freeze. It encouraged the whole family that people picked up on their needs and met them so freely.

In January, Gene and Wayne approached SANDY SILVIUS, a member of a Grace Church Bible study group. They asked her to consider leading a Bible study at Linda's home. Sandy's group was studying the "one another" verses in the New Testament. The verses from Romans said, "Be devoted to one another. . . . Honor one another. . . . Live in harmony with one another. . . . Stop passing judgment on one another. . . . Accept one another." After deciding to visit Linda, Sandy had said, "What a practical way to live those verses out."

The Bible study had fifteen members who discussed what meeting with Linda would mean. "It's not just a time commitment," Sandy warned. "It also includes clothing, hair, food, and scents." Many in the group were enthusiastic, and ten members decided to meet with Linda and Suzi every other Saturday. As the time approached for the first visit, apprehension fluttered through the group. They knew Linda was really fragile, and no one wanted to be the cause of a medical crisis. On the other hand, visitors had reported Linda's excitement at their willingness to come.

As the group prepared for their first meeting, Linda watched a For Sale sign go up in a neighbor's yard. Suzi had built an aviary in her tiny room, so Linda could enjoy watching the birds when she was too sick to be out of bed. She'd also built an aquarium in the wall. "It's my twenty-four-hour television," Linda joked. It had been almost two years since she first got sick.

Linda's mom had located an all-metal German telephone from the 1940s in an antique shop. The plastic shells of modern telephones made Linda react violently, as did televisions, tapes, tape recorders, and computers. Her family had also located and installed a metal intercom at the house to allow her more interaction with the family.

No MATTER HOW HARD THEY WORKED to create a safe environment inside, the outside world pushed in. A notice that the house next door had sold and would be fumigated sent Suzi into a panic. Linda's doctors confirmed that chemicals in the pesticides would wreak havoc on Linda—and could prove fatal. A week of searching for a safe place turned up nothing. It appeared that Linda would have to check into the Dallas hospital, an expense they could not afford. The Hermosa Beach house would not be safe for four months.

Word of the Harry family's search for a chemically free house for Linda and Suzi spread through the church. "I've got an old house up by Lake Elsinore," the church choir director told Suzi when she answered the phone. "You're welcome to it; but I'll warn you, it's very rustic. No carpet or synthetics or paint. There's nothing around for miles."

"Yes!" Suzi practically shouted. "How did you know?"

"Someone shared your need in choir. Stay as long as you like."

Lake Elsinore was the answer to Suzi's dilemma. The old ranch house with its three outbuildings sat on 350 wilderness acres in the foothills next to the lake. No one had lived there for years, and now it was up to Suzi to convert the old place. She chose the largest of the three outbuildings. Its lack of wiring, wallpaper, paint, and carpet made it ideal for Linda.

Suzi covered the holes in the walls with duct tape so the wind didn't blow through. Then she scheduled a work day. The members of the Bible study group from Grace Church quickly signed up. Others from the church also signed up to make the house livable. The work group would repair the roof; add a deck; and install doors, windows, and copper plumbing.

NIKKI CLINE, a member of the Bible study group, could hardly wait for the work day. The preacher at Grace Church had a unique way of looking at spiritual gifts that helped Nikki see where she could fit into Linda and Suzi's lives. One Sunday he had likened gifts to snowflakes. A person might have a thirty percent gift to teach and a twenty percent gift to help, while the next person may have thirty percent of this and thirty percent of that. Everyone has a different mixture so that each person has a unique place in the body of Christ. *If I am not fulfilling my part, and no one else can take my place, then the Body is not working right*, she believed.

Cindy had agreed that as long as her old van kept working, she would drive the group to Lake Elsinore, an hour farther from their church than the house in Hermosa Beach. Everyone had been anxious to finally meet Linda. "Good, they're outside," Sandy said as they pulled up to the cabin. They'd passed miles and miles of avocado ranches on their way. Nothing was even close except snakes, gophers, and rabbits.

"Hi, I'm Sandy," she said and then introduced the group to Linda, explaining, "We want to come twice a month if you're willing."

Linda seemed delighted with the idea, but Suzi was sending signals that she didn't want them there. While they visited, Suzi busied herself with food preparation and arranged the work party. "She's pretty unfriendly," someone said on the way home. "I thought she'd be glad to see us."

"It will work out," Sandy promised. Later Sandy learned that others had come, looked, and never come back. "We take being with others for granted—yet Linda was willing to be sick just for fellowship."

The second time the Bible study group arrived in the old van, Sandy could tell Suzi was flabbergasted. As Sandy lived up to her commitment to arrive twice a month, a friendship developed between the women. Sandy took Linda's health struggles to heart and felt responsible for everyone's consistency in using products that did not cause Linda to react. Sometimes group members seemed to think, *one time won't matter.* If Sandy noticed, she would ask the person not to go that time. "Perfume is not such a big deal" one person said. Sandy was kind but firm. "It is when it's Linda."

Gene was becoming a good friend too. He seemed to know just what to do. Suzi had quit her job; the two sisters were alone at the isolated cabin. Gene offered them his large dog for protection and company.

From the beginning, Gene realized that some people could not understand the experience of Linda and her family. Chemical sensitivities and immune reactions were something few people knew much about. Because the disability was invisible, many people misunderstood the situation. Both Suzi and Linda struggled with people's responses to Linda's illness. Persons showed their irritation through criticism of Linda, Suzi, the choice of treatment, and their lifestyle.

Some promoted miracle cures. Sensitive by nature and with no reserves to bounce back, the comments wounded Linda deeply.

Still reeling over expenses, pain, and loss of control, Linda received word that a tragic bus accident had claimed the lives of many of the doctors and nurses she had served with on an overseas mission. "Why them and not me?" Linda cried out to Gene. "These people had reached the pinnacle of what I wanted to achieve. They've left children behind who are now orphans. Here I am in total isolation; my condition is worsening, and they are killed. I can't do anything; my life is useless. Why didn't God take me instead?"

Gene shook his head. He saw possibilities in Linda that no one else saw—not even Linda herself. "Spiritual health comes from giving, Linda. Everyone has a purpose. We're not here by accident. Just being pleasant to a nurse can be a testimony. Look for those kinds of service you can or could provide. I think God is preparing you for something." Linda was uncertain, although she had faint glimpses that people saw possibilities in her.

On another afternoon Gene told her, "God can use you right where you are. You know, Linda, God has uniquely gifted you. I know that you have been praying for our ACAMPAR group. We want you to publish a prayer letter each month too."

"I'll think about it," Linda promised. Her mind was still active, and it felt good to have someone treat her as a capable person, encouraging her to explore reasonable opportunities. Linda did not know it yet, but she was already on a journey that was preparing her to use her gifts.

JONI EARECKSON TADA, a well-known author and speaker, had recently moved to the West Coast and was attending Grace Church. Joni had broken her neck in a 1967 diving accident that had left her a quadriplegic. When Bill Harry shared Linda's story and the family's discouragement, Joni nodded in understanding. When he had finished speaking, she asked Bill to talk to Linda about sharing some of her learning. Joni had begun Joni and Friends Ministries, an organization of Christian outreach to hurting persons. Bill agreed to talk to Linda about helping. She had always enjoyed helping others in overseas missions. Perhaps she could use her illness to reach others right here at home.

As Linda contemplated the possible good that could come of her suffering, others continued to visit faithfully. Cindy had watched Suzi and Linda survive at Lake Elsinore in their rugged surroundings. For a time they had no running water, no plumbing, and no electricity.

While Cindy trimmed Suzi and Linda's hair, she talked about the new perspectives their simple lifestyle had given her. "If you guys lived in pioneer days, you would survive. You've showed me that you don't have to have a lot of things to be happy." Cindy was experiencing some physical problems too. Without minimizing her own situation, she was able to look at them and realize, *Linda and her family are surviving. I can get through this too.*

A FIRE THAT ALMOST DESTROYED THE ELSINORE AREA and burned right up to the property line where Linda and Suzi lived, was fought with petrochemicals. They had no choice but to return to the Hermosa Beach house. Linda's doctors warned her to stay inside. The chemicals that had been sprayed four months earlier on their neighbor's home were still toxic to Linda. The doctor's words, *You'll have to find a place that's safe for Linda* echoed in Suzi's ears as she and Sandy scoured the California coast searching for a home.

Suzi began to drop by USC Medical Center to visit Sandy while her mother cared for Linda. Sandy realized how much concern and worry Suzi kept to herself rather than burdening her parents. "Say anything you want," Sandy encouraged Suzi. Sandy discovered that beneath her serious caregiving side, Suzi was funny and creative.

Suzie and Sandy began to go to movies or out to dinner, doing all the things Suzi could not do with Linda. Suzi had been "on duty" taking care of her sister for a long time without a real vacation. Sandy could tell that her new friend needed a break, so she offered to take care of Linda while Suzi got away for a while.

Sandy had stayed the night a couple of times and knew Linda's routine. All five of them—Bill, Margaret, Suzi, Linda, and Sandy—talked it over. They all agreed that Sandy would learn to give Linda her injections, safeguard her during loss of consciousness, and prepare her food. Suzi took a well-deserved rest. Suzi, glad for some time away, worried that all was going well at home.

"We had the greatest time," Sandy told Suzi, when she returned. The unexpected bonus for Sandy had been the development of her relationship with Bill and Margaret Harry, whom she found to be both gentle and kind. Sandy came from a totally dysfunctional family. Through her relationship with the Harrys, she realized God had given her a functional, loving family. "You know," Sandy told Suzi and Linda as they relaxed in Linda's room, "when God has something for you, the Lord nurtures it. It's incredible. If you act on your gut feeling, it literally changes your life. Your mom and dad have become my mom and dad."

IN THE SPRING OF 1980, THREE YEARS AFTER THE DIAGNOSIS, the Harry family agreed that the rustic wood cabin Suzi had found in the clean air around Santa Barbara, California, would be ideal for Linda. Sandy decided to move with the sisters. Bill and Margaret would remain in Hermosa Beach while Bill continued to work. The Bible study group members were committed to helping Linda wherever she went. They were willing and available to get the cabin in shape. Again, they helped foil the walls, strip the floors down to the hardwoods and varnish them, install a metal tub, and lay in a stock of exotic food. Men from Grace Church installed new electrical wiring with Mr. Harry.

Friends who wanted a close relationship with Linda had to consider their rights to wear nail polish, to have their hair permed, or to wear aftershave. Those sacrifices seemed small in order to see someone at a moment's notice. Linda's supporters had found that the requirement to be "permanently inconvenienced" was a real test of their servanthood. They came to understand that most of us want to give when and if it suits us. True yielding requires that we sacrifice some of our own comfort and convenience.

MANFRED SCHNEIDER, a member of Grace Church who was also a plumber, had heard about Linda and the Bible-writing outreach. When a respected church member asked him to install plumbing at the Santa Barbara cabin, he agreed. Both Manfred and his wife, Sharron, prepared for the work by becoming scent free, using special products and foregoing the use of perfumed products. The work project seemed like an adventure.

The love of family and friends for Linda deeply impressed Sharron. It bothered her that Linda and Suzi had to live in these surroundings. While the work of installing plumbing and getting the cabin ready lasted only a few weeks, the relationship with Sharron and Manfred continued. They decided they would commit to a scent-free lifestyle. They agreed to avoid the foods that caused Linda to react. In that way, they could develop a long-term relationship while being available to Linda in case an emergency arose.

WHAT'S A TRANSFER FACTOR?" Sandy asked, when the sisters explained that Linda had been accepted for experimental treatment in Dallas—treatment that might lessen some of Linda's violent reactions. It might allow her to live a less restricted life. Linda's condition had deteriorated so much in the last few years that doctors held no other hope for effective treatment.

"This is confusing, but I have a lymphocyte count of between zero to fifteen. Most people have a count of four to five thousand. Because I have so few T cells, my immune system is out of control and overreacts to most substances. With the transfer factor, technicians pass donated blood through a dialysis machine to extract the large T lymphocytes. They freeze-dry them to destroy the cell wall, which reduces incompatibility problems. Then they fractionate them and inject them into the patient. For me, it should allow my body to fight viruses, which is something it can't do right now, as well as stimulate production of T lymphocytes in my bone marrow."

"I want to fly with you," said Sandy, who was sitting on the wooden floor of Linda's foiled bedroom.

"That would be wonderful," Linda agreed. Suzi planned to drive to Dallas and set up an environmentally safe camp for Linda on a friend's property outside of Dallas. The goal was for Linda to receive the transfer factor as an outpatient of the hospital while living in a somewhat protected environment to see if the treatment was effective.

A seminary friend in Dallas had agreed to coordinate the six needed blood donors through the course of the treatment, thus relieving the family of that worry. Doctors explained it could take a year of treatments before they could determine if the treatment was helping Linda. Treatments might continue for years before Linda could reenter the twentieth-century's bombardment of chemicals and survive.

As Linda and Sandy boarded an airplane, Suzi and their friend, Nikki, began the three-day drive to Dallas. "I'm glad you're going with me," Suzi said, as they sped across southern California.

Nikki had identified two of her spiritual gifts: helping and giving. And when she met people who needed those gifts, she gave them. She'd learned of Linda's Dallas trip and of Suzi's trip by car, and she'd simply said, "Hey, Suzi, why don't I go with you?" They figured the length of the trip, a day to get the tent set up and the site prepared, and then Nikki would fly back to Dallas, using only a portion of her vacation time.

When Nikki had arrived at the cabin, Suzi had the little Volkswagen Rabbit loaded. An attached trailer was crammed full with three oxygen tanks, three five-gallon water tanks, the tent, clothing, cooking utensils, and sleeping bags. The two women had many things to talk about as they rode along. As they set up the tent after their third day on the road, Nikki realized that the key to their relationship was more than acceptance. Now and in future years she would see church groups that would "accept" Linda, but few were willing to be the least bit uncomfortable in order to make her comfortable. Many would be willing to have Linda come and sit outside while listening to the service. Most were not willing to come outside and sit with her— ever. The fourth day came so quickly it was hard to believe that it was time to go home.

"Thanks for coming," Suzi said, waving to Nikki as she ran to board her plane for Los Angeles.

Nikki stopped, "No. *Thank you*! I didn't think it would be this much fun."

The Harry family affected Nikki's life. Gene had said that just being pleasant to a nurse can be a testimony. The way the Harry family responded to Linda's great need had been a testimony to Nikki. Their faith in God had not wavered. They became instrumental in her life as an example of perseverance and trusting in the Lord in all circumstances. Margaret Harry had cared for Linda while Suzi worked. She had helped prepare her food and searched for the special items that would make Linda's life comfortable. Bill had shared Linda's struggles with his church family and had worked to build a nontoxic environment for her.

Years later after Nikki had dropped out of the Harrys' life, the family continued to keep her in prayer. When she came back to visit, she was overwhelmed to see the tears in Mr. Harry's eyes.

"I've been holding you up to the Lord," he said.

Later when Nikki took steps of trust to give up her job and go back to school, she remembered that God had worked in Linda's life, and she knew she could trust God with her life. *I didn't think it would be this much fun.*

LINDA WAS JUST HOME FROM THE HOSPITAL. Plans to stay at Suzi's environmentally safe campsite had fallen through. Linda's reaction to the treatment had been so violent that the doctors kept her in the Dallas hospital for four months while she adjusted to the transfer factor and received respiratory and physical therapy.

Since the Dallas hospital could not mail experimental treatments, each week the Harrys met a stewardess friend at the airport. This friend hand carried the transfer factor to Los Angeles. Then the Harrys delivered it to their daughter.

At the six-month mark, the Harrys could tell it was working. Linda no longer reacted so strongly to virtually everything, and the amount of energy and concentration she had grew. The number of letters she wrote on behalf of Joni and Friends Ministries increased dramatically. Linda began with four letters a week and progressed to several hundred letters a week. Later Linda wrote a counseling notebook for Joni and Friends. She was discovering that as she searched the scriptures her church members had painstakingly written for her, she could find a word of comfort for others and pass it along.

LOUIS KIENITZ had read the book *Joni*, the story of Joni Eareckson Tada's life after she broke her neck in a diving accident and became a quadriplegic. He had retired at age sixty-five and wanted to do something in the Lord's service. After reading Joni's book, Louis wrote to her at Joni and Friends Ministries. When Joni moved to the West Coast and joined the church Linda's parents attended, Louis received a letter from Joni telling him about Linda. Louis, touched by Linda's struggles, sent her a Christmas card. Linda wrote back and told him about people's writing the Bible for her.

"I'll be happy to write for you too," he said in his next letter. Linda sent him a long letter and included three pamphlets, then four more to transcribe in pencil.

"I'd be glad to do books," Louis wrote her when he returned the pencil-written pages. A handwritten copy of a Chuck Swindoll book arrived in a week. In a thank-you letter, Linda told him, "A lot of people start and quit after three chapters or so." Not Louis. He always finished what he started, and he offered to copy another book.

At first, believing Linda was in a hurry to have the books copied, he copied six hours each day. When Linda learned how much time he was devoting to it, she wrote and told him that he was doing too much. Now Louis copies books two hours each morning.

"I consider it my work the Lord sent me to do," wrote Louis, who has copied 8,000 pages for Linda. "I always had a hankering to do writing. In my life there were a number of years I was not doing anything. I felt so restless, so dissatisfied and useless." His copying for Linda has filled such a void in his own life that he wrote to Joni to suggest that she alert others to this ministry for the chemically sensitive people listening to her radio show.

As they corresponded, Louis became aware of the tremendous expenses that add up with environmental illness and chose to send money for a time. Through the years, they have maintained a friendship; first through letters and now Linda calls to talk.

While Linda was connecting with others and receiving their help, something was happening. The tide was turning, and she was being transformed into a powerful helper herself.

Linda was doing lots of writing and was thinking about starting some kind of organization to help other families connect with resources for their disabled family members. "It frustrates me to be unable to give people the information they require to meet their needs," she told a friend, while filing papers away.

"You need an office so you can get organized" he responded, and then built it for her.

Linda's office created a place where she could begin to work seriously at compiling a resource library to link people to the resources they need. It had been eight long years since she had been plunged so frighteningly into the world of disability. She told her family, "I want people to have a place to go when they are out of answers, when they have exhausted all their resources. I want to develop an organization that is an advocate for families. When people are stressed by taking care of life-and-death struggles, there is no time or energy to find the help that will remarkably change their life. I'll name the organization Direct Link and work to educate, inform, and advocate. I'll make it everything I wish we had had when I was first sick."

During her long illness, she came to some new understandings that she recorded for an article in the April 1980 *Moody* magazine.

When I moved to Oregon, I prayed I'd not just pursue my career and establish myself, but I'd get to know God better. One night, I lay awake, saying, "That I may know him," from Phil. 3:10 over and over. My focus was clear then; but the pain, heartache, and frustration of the last four years had clouded it.

Recently I came across the verse again and rediscovered the last part: "That I may know Him and the power of His resurrection and the fellowship of His sufferings, being conformed to His death." I had pleaded for the first part, unaware of the rest. The words hit me like a bolt of lightning. How could I know Him, really know Him, apart from His power and fellowship?

I would never really need His power if I were happily in full control of everything: that was easy to see. . . .

God is comfort. In all my affliction [God] is with me so that I may comfort others with the comfort . . . given me. Each crushing pressure I've been through these last years has removed all trust in myself or anything else. God's comfort makes me able to stand up inside, not fainting under the pressures I face.

With Gene's encouragement, Linda had taken that first step of outreach as a prayer coordinator for ACAMPAR. It had impressed on her the importance of giving back. Through that group, she discovered how many hurting families didn't know where to go for help. It was a dream come true when Direct Link acquired funding through the Department of Health and Human Services to develop a database.

As word of the organization spread, Direct Link for the disAbled, Inc. began to receive calls from people with a variety of disabilities and health-related questions. No matter what the need, Direct Link sought to help them find answers, because those involved knew what it was like to have no answers.

Even on the days when Linda was extremely weak, Sandy would hear Linda on the telephone, always willing to spend the time, to risk her own health and energy to find solutions for others. Linda would always hug everyone even though it might wipe her out later. She'd spend hours on the phone talking to a woman whose child was disabled and then spend several more hours searching for every possible bit of helpful information.

When Linda would begin to fade out, Sandy would suggest, "Don't do so much."

But Linda reminded her, "I have a right to do this."

THE UNDERSTANDING THAT BEING ALLOWED TO GIVE IS CRUCIAL has created opportunities for many people at Direct Link. Linda started a volunteer program at Direct Link as needs grew but finances did not. Robert is a volunteer with spina bifida who was always at home. He answers the telephone for Direct Link and inputs information into the computer. Martha always had her head down. Many persons believed her to be severely learning disabled. As a volunteer for Direct Link, she has become a whiz on the computer and is blooming.

Since its founding in 1986, Direct Link has grown each year. Direct Link helped nearly 400 persons in its first year, increasing to 6,414 persons in 1992. Linda's dream of connecting hurting families to information and resources was coming true.

Late one afternoon as she worked to pull resources together for a family flying to California for treatment, Linda wracked her brain for a place for them to stay. Everything else—transportation, hospital, physicians—was in place. She remembered the pencil-written Bible that Grace Church had presented to her. It had brought her through her darkest years and opened the door for her church to minister to her and her family. Gene had offered fellowship and an opportunity to give something back through ACAMPAR, Joni had urged her to use her suffering to help others too. Jan, Cindy, Sandy, Don and Annette, Nikki, Manfred and Sharron, Louis, and so many others had helped her family to endure and had provided for their needs. *Everybody needs an opportunity to give*, she thought as she dialed a nearby church.

"A family flying in from out of town needs a place to stay," she told the minister, explaining the need for housing.

"Of course. Leave it to me. I know just the family to help them," the minister said, promising to make the needed arrangements.

When she had finished the call, Linda made a note on the incoming family's file; turned out her desk lamp; and leaned back in her chair, happy to have made the contact and provided assistance. She had found her place.

EPILOGUE

It has been seventeen years since Linda was first diagnosed with vasculitus secondary to immune defects. The transfer factor and her church changed her life. Now she is able to work at Direct Link offices.

She cannot go into stores, but she can window-shop. She is functioning. She can go to church if she sits on the very back row.

Both Suzi and Sandy have returned to full-time work. Suzi serves as a resource specialist at Direct Link. Sandy works as a cook at a Santa Barbara school for the developmentally disabled and serves on the board of Direct Link. The three women live together in a normal house that was carefully built and sealed with a nontoxic sealer. The house has no foil in it. Her parents, Bill, now eighty and Margaret seventy-eight, moved to Santa Barbara three years ago and volunteer their time with Direct Link. ❖

Appendix 1

Guidelines for Helping

WE ARE PEOPLE, NOT STATISTICS; but numbers give us a sense of how many lives are affected by a disability. According to the National Organization on Disability (N.O.D.), the only national disability network organization concerned with all disabilities, all age groups and all disability issues, more than forty million people in the United States have physical or mental disabilities.

❖ As a caring friend you may want to suggest keeping records from the start. Parents of a child newly diagnosed with a disability may be too overwhelmed to consider getting organized with a notebook—or have any idea of what they should be writing down. The book, *The Futures of Children*, by Nicholas Hobbs, suggests that parents keep the following data: entries of names, addresses, phone numbers, dates of visits, the persons present during the visits, and as much of what was said as you can remember. Record the questions you asked, and the answers you received. Record any recommendations made. Make records of phone calls too; include the dates, the purpose, the result. It is best to make important requests by letter. Keep a copy for your notebook. Such documentation for every step of your efforts to get your child the service he [or she] needs can be the evidence which finally persuades a program director to *give* what he [or she] needs.

❖ As friends of the parents, you may want to help locate parents' organizations and programs. Provide childcare while both parents evaluate programs together.

❖ As a friend, you may wish to offer some assistance with studying or school projects. You will need to follow parent/teacher suggestions on the "best" way to work with the child.

❖ As a friend to a caregiver, listening to a problem is one way of beginning to solve it. Considering the solutions to similar problems offer clues to ways of solving the problem.

Talking about Disability
A Guide to Appropriate Language

1. Do not refer to a person's disability unless it is relevant.
2. Use the word *disability* rather than *handicap* to refer to a person's disability.
3. Avoid referring to people with disabilities as "the disabled, the deaf, epileptics, the retarded, a quadriplegic," and so forth. Use descriptive terms as adjectives, not as nouns.
4. Avoid negative or sensational descriptions of a person's disability. Don't say, "suffers from," "a victim of," or "afflicted with." Don't refer to people with disabilities as "patients" unless they are receiving treatment in a medical facility. Never say "invalid."
5. Don't portray people with disabilities as overly courageous, brave, special, or superhuman. This implies that it is unusual for people with disabilities to have talents or skills.
6. Don't use *normal* to describe people who don't have disabilities. It is better to say "people without disabilities" or "typical," if necessary to make comparisons.
7. Never say "wheelchair-bound" or "confined to a wheelchair." People who use mobility or adaptive equipment are, if anything, afforded freedom and access that otherwise would be denied them.
8. Never assume that a person with a communication disorder (speech impediment, hearing loss, motor impairment) also has a cognitive disability, such as mental retardation. On the other hand, people with mental retardation often speak well.

—Coalition for Tennesseans with Disabilities

Communicating with the Alzheimer Patient

COMMUNICATION IS A COMMON PROBLEM associated with AD. The affected individual may be unable to make herself understood or may be unable to understand others. If you are having problems communicating with someone who has AD, first make sure that he or she is not suffering from a hearing impairment.

In the early stages of the disease, enable communication by using signs, labels, or written messages that can reassure the individual. Assume that your loved one can understand more than she can express. Never talk about her as if she were not there.

As the disease progresses, your loved one will be less able to communicate; and eventually, may be unable to speak. Nonverbal communication, such as touch or laughter, may be more useful then. The person with AD can understand nonverbal communication and humor much longer than he can understand spoken communication. Communicate affection by touch.

Below are some suggestions to help you get the message across:
1. Be calm and supportive. Maintain eye contact and use touch to reassure him and show that you are listening.
2. Show your interest in what she is saying or feeling.
3. Pay attention to his voice and gestures for clues to what he is feeling. Sometimes his emotions are more important than what he is trying to say.
4. If you don't understand what she is trying to say, let her know and encourage her to point or gesture.
5. If he cannot find a word, offer a guess.
6. If she uses the wrong word and you know what she means, supply the correct word. If this upsets her, do not correct future mistakes.
7. If he is upset and cannot explain verbally, offer comfort and reassurance. Trying to get him to explain may make him more upset.

—Alzheimer's Association

Communicating with Persons
Who Are Hard-of-Hearing

1. Come closer. Shortening the distance between speaker and
    listener will increase the loudness of sound. This approach to
    improving communication is much more effective than
    "raising" your voice. You should never shout at a person who
    is hard of hearing. Some hearing aid users are especially
    sensitive to loudness.
2. Turn off the radio, or television, or running water, or air
    conditioner. These sounds are amplified by a hearing aid and
    interfere with communication.
3. Talk face to face. Speak at eye level. Don't chew gum, smoke,
    talk behind a newspaper, or cover your mouth while you are
    speaking. Also, make sure the movements of your lips and
    facial expressions are clearly visible.
4. Try rewording a message. At times the person may be par-
    tially dependent on speechreading (also known as lipread-
    ing), because some sounds may not be easily heard even with
    a hearing aid. Since some words are easier to speechread than
    others, rephrasing a message may make it easier for the
    person to understand.
5. Show special awareness. Call the person by name to initiate
    communication. Give a frame of reference for the discussion
    by mentioning the topic at the outset. Be patient, particularly
    when the person is tired or ill and may be less able to hear.
6. Extend extra consideration in a group situation. Only one
    person should be talking at a time. Also, alert the person who
    is hard of hearing to changes in speakers.

—**Alexander Graham Bell Association for the Deaf, Inc.**

Special Needs Created by Environmental Illness

PERSONS WITH ENVIRONMENTAL ILLNESS CANNOT TOLERATE substances in their environment that most persons consume, breathe, cover themselves with, or live in each day. Here are some of the needs of persons with environmental illness:

1. Public understanding. The disease is real, however baffling. It isn't "all in their heads" nor can they "snap out of it."
2. Financial help. Many patients have incurred medical bills over the years and face great obstacles in getting disability benefits. Help finding nontraditional or safe work.
3. Nontoxic housing. Renovated homes and trailers constructed of porcelain over steel have reduced patients' suffering.
4. Nontoxic land. Housing must be on land free of pesticides, drifting smoke, air pollution, and auto exhaust.
5. Support of friends and family. Persons who respect their sensitivities by not wearing perfume, perfumed soap, shampoo, aftershave, cosmetics and deodorants, synthetic fibers, or dry-cleaned clothing.

Other ways you can help:

❖ Share your recycled, chemical-free 100 percent cotton or silk clothing.
❖ Share your chemical-free garden produce.
❖ Help raise funds to provide medical equipment for a patient.
❖ Lobby for a cleaner environment.
❖ Use alternative, less toxic methods of pest control.
❖ Visit or phone lonely and isolated environmentally ill patients.

Share, Care and Prayer Ministries
905 North First Avenue
Arcadia, CA 91006

Caring Skills Inventory

EVERYONE HAS A GIFT TO SHARE. Below is a checklist of opportunities for caring developed by Love Inc. Along with the participant's name, address, telephone number and age, the form requests available hours—either morning, afternoon, or evening and specific days available. A note informs volunteers, "If you are unable to help when called upon, you may simply decline that particular request."

- ❖ Assist with shopping 1 or 2 times a month
- ❖ Transport people to medical appointments 1 or 2 times a month
- ❖ Transport furniture in your truck
- ❖ Deliver food occasionally with adequate notice
- ❖ Call people who are depressed, anxious, lonely, etc. and need a listening ear
- ❖ Visit shut-ins, elderly, disabled (__) once, (__) more often
- ❖ Provide respite care
- ❖ Do yard work for disabled and elderly
- ❖ Provide auto maintenance/repair, plumbing, carpentry, electrical work/repair, painting
- ❖ Be a Church Partner (call, pick up if necessary, be with two or three times, and introduce to others in your church)
- ❖ Counsel on money management
- ❖ Assist people with filling out various forms
- ❖ Help someone with meal planning
- ❖ Give medical assistance (paramedic, nurse, MD)
- ❖ Counsel on medical arrangements (walk through with a person facing a specific illness)
- ❖ Give legal assistance
- ❖ Give dental assistance
- ❖ Tutor (Circle: adults / children / other: _____.)
- ❖ Translate: Language _____
- ❖ Sign for (persons who are) deaf
- ❖ Provide temporary baby-sitting or child care
- ❖ Donate (circle: baby supplies / furniture / _____)
- ❖ Give financial aid (for rent, utility bills, medicine, etc.)

Parents Helping Parents Do and Don't List For Visiting Parents (Peer Counselors)

PARENTS HELPING PARENTS IS A NATIONALLY RECOGNIZED non-profit volunteer group of parents, professionals, and lay counselors who are sensitive to the problems and concerns of families with children having special needs.

Things to do:

❖ Let them (the family members to whom you are talking) direct the conversation by encouraging them to express their concerns and their questions.

❖ Be open-minded and accepting of their feelings and attitudes.

❖ Be a good listener. Confidentiality is a must.

❖ Acknowledge and talk to and about the other children in the family.

❖ Ask about the other parent and how he or she is doing if he or she is not present.

❖ Ask the parent how he or she is doing. Especially, ask how the mother is recovering from the birthing process.

❖ Act as a friend and share similar feeling, fears, apprehension, etc.

❖ Boost morale and self-image; that is, comment on positive steps that they have already taken.

❖ Tactfully relate your own positive experiences, but allow them to find their own solutions.

❖ Inform them of supportive services relative to their child's disability but don't overload them with information at first, as they may feel threatened.

❖ Encourage parents to take time out for themselves; with a view toward balance in caring for and meeting the needs of all the family members.

❖ Agree with them that this is a terrible thing that has happened to them and their child. (Not that the child is a terrible thing.)

❖ Find something about the child that allows you to make a positive or complimentary statement. (curly hair, great skin, sleeping well, crying—has good lungs, etc.)

Things not to do:

❖ Do not give medical advice.
❖ Do not try to psychoanalyze.
❖ Do not try to provide final answers or solutions. You may tell what you have done, but let them reason things out. You may try to present various alternatives.
❖ Do not overpower them.
❖ Do not "rundown" professionals, agencies, or institutions of care.
❖ Do not "dump" your problems on them.
❖ Do not take on their problem.
❖ Do not "talk about them" to others.
❖ Do not share medicines.

A Letter to Family and Friends
Practical Suggestions from a Parent

THIS LETTER FROM KATHY HUNTER, president and founder of the International Rett Syndrome Association, is one that clearly states ways family and friends can connect in meaningful, helpful ways when a child has a disability. Many of the suggestions apply to other disabilities and age groups. Rett syndrome is a neurological disorder characterized by early loss of acquired behavioral, social and psychomotor skills. Here, are Kathy Hunter's suggestions:

❖ *Don't be afraid to ask about our daughter. We have spent many hours with specialists to learn about her condition. It helps to know that you are interested.*

❖ *Respect our decisions about her care. We have listened carefully to the recommendations of doctors and therapists, and have based our decisions on what we feel to be the best for her.*

❖ *Treat our daughter as a part of the family. Include her in the children's activities. She may not be able to do everything that the others do, but it is important that she does take part. Nothing hurts more than having your child overlooked because she is different.*

❖ *Teach your children about her. Explain her condition in terms they can understand. Tell them it is all right to ask questions. Ten questions are better than one stare. When your children see that you treat her first as a child, they will respond in the same way.*

❖ *Don't forget to say hello. Although she cannot talk, she does love to be spoken to. It may take her a moment to respond, but she will. Good things come to those who wait.*

❖ *Please understand that family gatherings, particularly birthday parties, can be very difficult at times. No matter how accepting we are, we still agonize for the milestones our daughter will not achieve. With time, the pain will ease. Try to be sensitive.*

❖ *Ask if you can help once in a while. Don't be surprised if we don't accept your offer at first, however. It is hard to let others help when society has taught us that as special parents, we have to do everything "special." Keep asking until we let you help. It isn't that we don't need the help; it's just that we don't want to burden you if your offer is not sincere.*

❖ *Offer to care for our daughter sometime so that we can get away together. Remember that everything we do and everywhere we go is much more complicated that the ordinary. There is no such thing as sleeping in on Sunday morning or any morning.*

❖ *Offer to feed our daughter at the next family gathering. It does not take a special technique that you do not have, nor will she eat better for us. It will be a good break for her and for us.*

❖ *Don't leave our daughter out when you buy gifts for the children. If the gift is something she cannot chew or a toy she cannot play with, find something that she can be happy with.*

❖ *Don't tell us that we were specially "chosen" for this child. We are ordinary people who are striving against sometimes extraordinary circumstances to provide a "normal" family life. We were not singled out for the job. It just happened at our house. It could just as easily happen at yours, and you would carry on as we have, like ordinary loving parents who care.*

❖ *Don't underestimate the power of your caring. Everything you do to try to understand will help more than you will ever know.*

Appendix 2

Print Resources

Bryant, Charles V. 1991. *Rediscovering Our Spiritual Gifts: Building Up the Body of Christ through the Gifts of the Spirit.* Nashville, TN: Upper Room Books.
A practical look at how the gifts of the Holy Spirit can renew the lives of individuals and revitalize the church's ministry. Call 800-972-0433.

Durback, Robert. 1989. *Seeds of Hope,* A Henri Nouwen Reader. New York, NY: Bantam Books.
A selection of Henri Nouwen's finest work on such diverse topics as intimacy, loneliness, success, prayer, compassion, and God; as well as the insatiable human need for joy, peace, and love. Call 800-223-6834.

Geralis, Elaine. 1991. *Children with Cerebral Palsy: A Parent's Guide* Woodbine House, 5615 Fishers Lane, Rockville, MD 20852
Provides information on diagnosis, medical treatments, early intervention, adjustment, family life, legal rights, assessment, therapies, special education, daily care, and advocacy. Call 800-843-7323.

Hunter, Kathy, ed. 1992. *Bridges: A Book of Hope and Inspiration for Families.* International Rett Syndrome Association. (See Appendix 3 for address and phone number.)
The shared experiences of parents with a child diagnosed with Rett syndrome.

Jones, Ron. 1990. *The Acorn People.* New York, NY: Bantam Books.
The adventures of a group of youth in wheelchairs, who are attending a summer camp together. Call 800-223-6834.

Kriegsman, Kay, et. al. 1992. *Taking Charge: Teenagers Talk about Life and Physical Disabilities.* Woodbine House (see address above). Call 800-843-7323.
How to handle remarks, stress; how to help family and friends recognize one's individuality first and disability second.

202 ❖ THE COURAGE TO CARE

Kupfer, Fern. 1988. *Before & after Zachariah: A True Story about a Family and a Different Kind of Courage.* Chicago, IL: Academy Chicago Publishers.

One family's journey with their son, Zachariah, who has profound brain damage and their decision to place him in residential care.

Mace, Nancy L. and Peter V. Rabins. 1992, rev. ed. *The 36-Hour Day: A Family Guide to Caring for Persons with Alzheimer's Disease, Related Dementing Illnesses, and Memory Loss Later in Life.* New York, NY: Warner Books. Also available from The Alzheimer's Association, 800-272-3900.

Nelson-Morrill, Creston, ed. 1991. *The Florida Caregivers' Handbook: An Essential Resource Guide for Caregivers & Their Older Loved Ones.* HealthTrac Books, PO Box 13599, Tallahassee, FL 32317.

Caregivers from around the country will find the book useful. Includes a directory of services, the normal aging process, medication management, the nursing home decision, Medicare and Medicaid, power of attorney and guardianship, living will, financial planning, and ethics of caregiving.

Thornburgh, Ginny, ed. 1992. *That All May Worship: An Interfaith Welcome to People with Disabilities.*

Assists congregations, denominational groups, and seminaries to welcome people with disabilities into all aspects of worship and religious life. To order write the National Organization on Disability, 910 Sixteenth St. NW, Suite 600, Washington, DC.

Periodicals

The Accessible Home: Remodeling Concerns for the Disabled (leaflet) United Cerebral Palsy Associations, Inc.; 1522 K St. NW, Suite 1112; Washington, DC 20005-1202. Call 800-USA-5UCP.

Exceptional Parent: Parenting Your Child with a Disability (magazine), P.O. Box 3000 Dept. EP, Denville, NJ 07834. To subscribe: 800-247-8080.

Monthly magazine of articles covering various issues related to raising a child with a disability plus an Annual Guide to Products and Services and a special resource section.

Appendix 3

Organizations

International Rett Syndrome Association, 9121 Piscataway Rd., Clinton, MD 20735.

A nonprofit organization for parents, professionals, and others concerned with Rett syndrome. Provides an information and referral service and a support network with other parents. Encourages research for cause, control, and cure of Rett syndrome.

North American Riding for the Handicapped Association, Inc., P.O. Box 33150, Denver, CO 80233. Call 800-369-RIDE.

Therapeutic horseback riding centers for individuals with disabilities. Call for center locations.

National Organization for Rare Disorders, P. O. Box 8923, New Fairfield, CT 06812.

NORD, created to educate the general public and medical profession about the existence, diagnosis, and treatment of rare disorders and Orphan Drugs (therapies that alleviate symptoms of some rare diseases), acts as a clearinghouse of information. Networks families with similar disorders together for mutual support. Fosters communication among rare disease voluntary agencies, government, industry, researchers, academic institutions and concerned individuals. Provides a newsletter.

Alzheimer's Association, 919 North Michigan Ave., Chicago, IL 60611-1676, 800-273-3900.

National voluntary organization providing support and assistance to Alzheimer's patients and their families. Researches cause, treatment, and cure of Alzheimer's disease. Provides lists of local support groups and a catalog of helpful books and brochures.

Direct Link for the disAbled, P.O. Box 1036, Solvang, CA 93463.

A national organization with an extensive database linking local, state, and national resources for any disability, chronic illness, or rare disorder.

204 ❖ THE COURAGE TO CARE

The Alexander Graham Bell Association for the Deaf, 3417 Volta Place, NW; Washington, DC 20007.

A membership organization whose goal is the development of listening skills and spoken language in hearing impaired people, especially children. Provides newsletters, journals, conventions, conferences, lending library, and other membership benefits.

Parents Helping Parents (PHP), The National Center on Parent Directed Family Resource Centers, 535 Race St., Suite 140, San Jose, CA 95126, 800-397-9827.

Improves the life of children with special needs and their families by facilitating the development and expansion of Parent Directed Family Resource Centers. How-To Manuals provide detailed steps to get started, ongoing telephone consultations, and technical assistance. Call for a list of resources for replicating programs.

National Organization on Disability, 910 16th Street, NW, Suite 600; Washington, DC 20006, 800-695-0285.

Promotes the acceptance and full participation in all life's aspects, of America's forty-three million persons with physical, sensory, or mental disabilities through a network of 3,000 communities nationwide. Assists other national associations in promoting expanded opportunities for people with disabilities.

The N.O.D. Religion and Disability Program is an interfaith effort urging local congregations, national denominational groups, and seminaries to remove the obstacles to worship that alienate people with disabilities. Materials help religious communities identify and remove architectural, communications, and attitudinal barriers.

National Information Center for Children and Youth with Disabilities (NICHCY), P.O. Box 1492, Washington, DC 20013-1492; 800-695-0285.

NICHCY provides free information to assist parents, educators, caregivers, advocates, and others in helping children and youth with disabilities become participating members of the community. This national information and referral clearinghouse, supported through a cooperative agreement among the U.S. Dept. of Education, Office of Special Education, and Rehabilitative Services answers questions on all disability issues. Provides technical assistance to family and professional groups.

Mothers United for Moral Support, 150 Custer Ct., Green Bay, WI 54301.

Newsletter and international parent matching program for parents of children who are medically fragile or who have a rare disorder. Parent support groups, case advocacy, systems advocacy, education, and information.

Share, Care and Prayer Ministries, 905 North First Avenue, Arcadia, CA 91006.

Newsletter, clothing exchange, tape library, and Christian support group for persons with chemical sensitivities, environmental illness, pesticide poisoning, and other related issues. Members share experiences, tips on nontoxic products, and prayer requests.

The ARC, (formerly Association for Retarded Citizens of the United States), 500 E. Border St., S-300; Arlington, TX 76010.

A national organization committed to securing for all people with mental retardation the opportunity to choose and realize their goals of where and how they learn, live, work, and play. The ARC has more than 100 publications and videos available to anyone needing information on research, employment, prevention, family, and organizational issues.

Joni and Friends, 28720 Canwood Street, Agoura Hills, CA 91301.

National Library Services for the Blind and Physically Handicapped, 800-424-8567.

Provides audiocassette and record players, books, records, and audiotapes for persons who cannot read, hold, or turn the pages of a regular print book either short- or long-term. Records textbooks for students with special needs and referrals for other services.

United Cerebral Palsy Associations, 800-872-5827.

UCPA will also provide information for setting up a respite program.

National Head Injury Foundation, 800-444-NHIF.

American Paralysis Association/Spinal Cord Injury Hotline, 800-526-3456.

National Alliance for the Mentally Ill, 800-950-NAMI.

National Down Syndrome Congress, 800-232-NDSC.

For additional organizations, call NICHCY at 800-695-0285.

Judy Griffith Ransom

is a freelance writer and photographer whose work has appeared in numerous newspapers and magazines around the country. She is the author of *To Be the Hands of God*, a 1992 Upper Room book; *Blessings and Bible Stories from the Old Testament*, a 1993 Tradery House book; and the coauthor of *Open House: Recipes & Food Memories from the Culinary Community* for the National Alliance to End Homelessness.

Judy speaks to churches about creating more caring congregations and is a reader for a college student who has cerebral palsy. She lives with her family in Hendersonville, Tennessee. ❖